Sometimes
LIFE
SUCKS

Sometimes LIFE SUCKS

When someone you love dies

MOLLY CARLILE

ALLEN&UNWIN

First published in 2010

Allen & Unwin
83 Alexander Street
Crows Nest NSW 2065
Australia
Phone: (61 2) 8425 0100
Fax: (61 2) 9906 2218
Email: info@allenandunwin.com
Web: www.allenandunwin.com

Cataloguing-in-Publication details are available
from the National Library of Australia
www.librariesaustralia.nla.gov.au

ISBN 978 1 74237 188 7

Internal design by Benjamin Tan
Set in 11/15 pt Caslon by Midland Typesetters, Australia
Printed in Australia by McPherson's Printing Group

10 9 8 7 6 5 4 3 2 1

Mixed Sources

Product group from well-managed
forests, and other controlled sources
www.fsc.org Cert no. SGS-COC-004121
© 1996 Forest Stewardship Council

The paper in this book is FSC certified.
FSC promotes environmentally responsible,
socially beneficial and economically viable
management of the world's forests.

DEDICATION

To my husband, Will, and our kids, Sean, Lachlan, Em and her Johnny, for their patience, critical analysis and encouragement.

To my mum, Bernadette McPhee, for her guidance.

To Marie Carlile for her gentleness and support.

To my friend Patsi Graham (1950–2009), who listened attentively to some of these stories just days before she died.

To all the patients and families I have cared for over the years, who trusted me with their personal stories so that others may benefit.

To my nieces and nephews and the next generation of young people who are eager for knowledge and understanding, in the hope that they will improve the way society supports dying and grieving people in years to come.

CONTENTS

CONTENTS

INTRODUCTION

From the moment we are born we are constantly changing. We change, the world around us changes and the people we love and care about change. We grow, we learn new things, we make new friends and leave some old friends behind. We'll have times when we achieve great things and times of disappointment. We'll have times of joy and of terrible sadness. We'll have times when we are kind and when we are mean. We'll have times when we want to be hanging out with other people and when we just want to be alone. Change is the only thing that is always with us in life and yet when it happens we often feel scared, angry or ripped off. We expect life to be normal, whatever that is, but there's no such thing as normal. No one is always happy, healthy, surrounded by wonderful friends and family, rich, beautiful, young, successful. Life just isn't like that.

Instead life is more like a beach. Sometimes you can sit on the sand and it's warm, the sun is shining, birds are singing, the water is warm and calm and the sky is blue. On other days you might go to the beach and the sky is grey and cloudy, the cold wind is blowing the sand and stinging your legs, the waves are roaring and crashing on the rocks and there are no birds to be seen. The important thing is we need to experience the cold, stormy days to be grateful for the warm sunny ones. And it's the same with life. If we always got just what we wanted, we wouldn't value it. We need to feel sadness, anger and disappointment to appreciate happiness, joy and laughter.

When someone we love dies, we can think we'll never be happy again. We miss them and want them back. But as we begin to appreciate the life we lived with them, to remember the things about them that we loved, we will feel happy again. Happy remembering what they meant to us and in being able to share those memories with others.

Sometimes life sucks, but sometimes it's absolutely wonderful and I hope this book helps you to appreciate both. Being able to make sense of the feelings you have when someone close to you leaves, is very sick or dies helps you to know you're not weird. If you can get to know yourself better you will understand why you might be feeling angry, guilty, hurt or rejected.

If you can feel more relaxed talking about death and grief with your friends and other close people you will discover that there is no such thing as normal. Whatever you're thinking and feeling is OK, 'cause that's normal for you.

Finally, I hope this book helps you to value your life with all its ups and downs, joys and disappointments, moments of happiness and moments of sadness, so that you can help people around you who might be finding it hard.

Molly Carlile
To contact me or to find out about workshops or teaching resources, please go directly to my websites:
WWW.MOLLYCARLILE.COM, WWW.DEATHTALKER.COM

CHAPTER 1

WHEN FRIENDS DIE AND YOU'RE ON YOUR OWN — — —

Finn thought his heart would break when his little dog, Captain, was hit by a car. He cried quietly in bed at night for weeks on end, but that pain was nothing compared to how he felt right now. He couldn't believe that three of his mates were dead and his best friend, Toad, half dead in hospital. They had all gone to the party together, they were all drinking but, as usual, Dad had come and picked Finn up early 'cause he didn't trust him to come home with the rest of the guys. Now he was alone. People looked at him weird. He knew they were wondering why he hadn't been with the others. Finn didn't want anyone to know he was actually relieved that Dad had picked him up early, even though it was embarrassing. Dad had saved his life, but what life?

Finn, Church, Baz and Mouth had been mates since they all started kindergarten together. Toad had come along later in primary school and he and Finn had become best mates the day Toad had saved him from being beaten up by a gang of Grade 6 boys. Even when Finn thought about this now it made him laugh. Toad had saved him by blowing a 'power fart', which so impressed the big kids they forgot about Finn and gathered around Toad begging him to do it again. Toad's power farts became legendary.

He did them all through high school. He did them in class when the teacher was facing the board. He did them in school assembly. He did them when he was playing footy and there wasn't enough action down his end of the field. He even did them at parties in front of the girls, which Finn had tried to tell him wasn't going to get him a chick, but he did it anyway.

Finn and Toad did everything together. Of course they hung out with the other guys as well, but it was Toad who Finn trusted most of all. When Finn got with 'Smelly Sally' at the Year 9 Formal, Toad stirred him but he didn't tell the other guys. In fact Toad promised he'd never tell anyone as long as Finn told him all the gory details. Toad taught Finn how to drive, though his mum didn't know. Toad also got him his part-time job at the supermarket. And Toad had talked Finn's dad into letting him go to the party. Now Toad was in hospital and Mum said he was 'pretty well cactus' when she was telling Finn's sister about it on the phone.

Finn felt sick. He didn't know what to do and now, to make matters worse, Mouth's mum had come over last night and asked him if he would talk at Mouth's funeral. The whole time she was there Finn felt awkward. He didn't know what to say to her. She kept looking at him with her red, puffy eyes as if it was his fault.

DON'T WORRY
We often feel uncomfortable around grieving people because they are sad, and we imagine we are somehow to blame.

After she'd left Finn told his Mum that he didn't want to talk at Mouth's funeral 'cause he didn't know what to say.

'Just say some nice things about him, love. It doesn't have to go for ages. Just a few nice things about what a good friend he was,' she said.

Finn felt the tears welling up in his eyes and ran from the kitchen out the back door. He sat on the step and his scruffy old dog, Shaggy, came up and nuzzled his face. Finn put his arms around Shaggy and bit his lip to stop the tears. He thought about Captain and how much he'd missed him until one night Dad had brought Shaggy home with him from work. He wondered if one day when he was old, he'd have replaced Church, Baz and Mouth with new friends, like he'd replaced Captain. The thought made him angry: angry with himself; angry with the world. And then came the thought he'd been trying to push out of his mind since the night of the crash: *What if Toad dies too?* Or maybe worse still, *What if he's just a vegetable, can't think, can't talk, can't move?*

Mum came out and sat on the step next to Finn. She put her arm around him and gave him a squeeze.

'Life really sucks sometimes, love,' she said. 'If you don't want to talk at Mouth's funeral you don't have to. I'll call his mum and tell her if you like.'

'You can't do that, Mum, they already hate me 'cause I'm still alive.'

'Now listen to me, Finn,' said Mum. 'It's not your fault and I won't have you feeling guilty just because you did the right thing.'

'I DIDN'T do the right thing. I just stopped drinking earlier 'cause I knew Dad was coming to pick me up.'

'Well, none of you should have been drinking but the boys shouldn't have been in that car. For God's sake, Finn, none of them have a licence.'

'Oh SHUT UP, Mum. I KNOW!' he snapped.

WHAT CAN HELP
When someone says out loud what we're thinking it can make us feel angry. It can help to say you're feeling angry and talk about it.

Finn threw Shaggy off his lap and stormed into the backyard. He picked up the axe and started chopping away at the block of wood he'd left sitting by the woodpile yesterday. He expected Mum to call out to him to be careful but she didn't. He turned around and looked back towards the step—but she wasn't there. She'd gone inside. Finn didn't want to be mad at Mum 'cause he knew she was right. Thank God, she didn't know about all the nights they had gone out in Mouth's old paddock bomb, doing burn-outs and donuts in the supermarket carpark.

The day of Mouth's funeral came and Finn put on the suit Mum had bought him. Dad was waiting in the car. Finn sat on the end of his bed looking at last year's footy photo. There they all were: Mouth, Baz, Church, Finn and Toad. All with their arms folded, trying not to laugh. Toad had a strained look on his face 'cause he was trying to brew up a power fart timed for exactly the moment when the camera went off. Finn looked at the photo. He looked into each of his friend's faces, one by one. He tried to memorise their smiles. He imagined them talking to him. He would never hear those voices again. He had lost not just one but all of his friends. Friends he had spent his whole life with. Part of him wished he had been in the car too, so they could all have died together. As soon as he thought this, he felt bad. Who would be there to look out for Toad if he was dead as well? Just then Mum stuck her head around the door.

> 'When my best friend died I thought my future died too. But it didn't die, it just changed from what I'd imagined.'
> Laura, 16

'Right to go love?' she asked.

'I guess.'

The funeral was terrible. Finn hated seeing grown-ups crying. It made him feel helpless. And what was worse, he just couldn't cry. When he stood up to go out the front and talk about Mouth he felt the eyes of everyone on him except Mouth's dad, who wouldn't look at him at all. He couldn't remember what he said but he remembered kids from school standing by the road as the car with the coffin in it drove past. Then at the cemetery his teacher Mr Parkinson came up and put his hand on Finn's shoulder.

'You did a good job, Finn,' he said gently.

'A good job? A good, bloody job?' Finn snapped and stormed off towards the car.

What does he mean I did a good job? he thought. 'Parko's having a go just like everyone else. I'll never be able to show my face at school again. I'm the one who deserted his mates and lived.'

Finn slid down against the car and sat in the dirt. He picked up a stone and threw it as far as he could. 'Arrrr!' he yelled at no one in particular.

WHAT CAN HELP
When we feel frustrated and angry, energy builds up inside us. Sometimes this can make us feel like we're going to explode. Letting that energy go by doing something physical helps.

Church and Baz had a joint funeral. Finn didn't go. He just couldn't. Instead he waited till Mum and Dad had left and put on the DVD of his sixteenth birthday party. There they all were: Church, Baz, Mouth, Toad and Finn, dancing around like idiots to the Hilltop Hoods. Finn wondered what parties would be like in the future, without the boys. He wondered if he'd ever have a party again; if he'd ever feel happy again.

DON'T WORRY
When someone you love dies, you think you will never feel happy again. But slowly you'll start to notice yourself smiling at things that are funny. One day you'll realise that you feel happy, even though it might only last for a few minutes.

A couple of days later Finn was finally allowed to visit Toad in hospital. Toad's mum said it might help. Finn sat in the car as Mum drove into the city. He felt scared.

'What do you recon he'll look like, Mum?' Finn asked.

'I don't know, love, but he's still in intensive care, so I guess there'll probably be lots of tubes and machines and things,' she replied.

DID YOU KNOW?
When you are going to see someone who is badly injured or dying in hospital, it helps to know what to expect.

That was an understatement. Finn stood at the door of intensive care and stared. It was a big, white room full of machines. He looked around at the people in the beds. They all looked like robots or something: tubes, machines, poles with plastic bags full of different coloured water hanging from them. It wasn't like a normal hospital room. There were no flowers, no talking, no pictures on the wall. Finn froze. He didn't want to go in. Just when he was about to turn around and run back to the car, Toad's mum saw him and came rushing over.

'Thank God you're here, Finn,' she said and gave him a hug. There was no escape now.

She held Finn's hand and led him over to a bed in the very corner of the room. Finn realised the person in the bed must be Toad, but he didn't recognise him. His face was all puffy and bruised, his head was covered with so many bandages it looked like he was wearing a white beanie, and his eyes were swollen shut. There were tubes going into the side of his neck and wires coming from his chest to a machine, making a beeping sound, by the bed.

There was a big tube coming straight from his throat that looked like a vacuum cleaner hose and it was connected to a machine that kept making a loud sucking sound. Going straight through his leg were big silver wires that were suspended on a huge metal frame around the bed. His arm was plastered up to the shoulder and was hanging from a pole.

'Come around this side, Finn, you can sit on the chair,' Toad's mum said.

Finn looked around for his mum but she was standing in the doorway talking to Toad's dad. He had no choice. He walked carefully around the end of the bed to the other side. He sat on the chair next to Toad's mum. It was then he noticed. Where Toad's other arm should have been there was nothing. A big bandage across his shoulder ended in . . . nothing. A stump, that's all there was. He felt sick. This couldn't be Toad, it looked nothing like him. This was a battered body in a bed, missing an arm. Toad was a big, buff guy.

Finn looked the body up and down. *No, this can't be him. It's a mistake*, he thought.

But then he saw it: peeking out from under the bandage across his shoulder, the very top of a coloured tattoo. The head of 'Mr Toad'.

Thoughts whirled around in Finn's mind. It can't be him. It doesn't look like him. This guy is skinny. But then there was the Mr Toad tattoo. Finn knew no one else would be gutsy enough to get a tattoo of a children's book character on his shoulder and surely there was no one else who would choose Mr Toad. Why would they? It wouldn't make any sense.

'You OK there love?' asked Toad's mum as she put her hand on his shoulder.

Finn couldn't move. He didn't want to look again. No matter how much he tried to convince himself that this was all a terrible mistake, he knew it wasn't.

'It's pretty scary the first time, but you'll get used to it,' she said softly. 'He needs you, Finn.'

'What can I do?' Finn asked.

'Just sit here for a while and talk to him. He can hear you, you know,' she said.

Finn looked up and stared at Toad's mum.

'How can he possibly hear me?' he snapped.

'He just can, Finn, so please . . . talk to him,' she said, and it sounded like she was pleading. She got up from the chair and walked away.

WHAT CAN HELP
Sometimes telling someone about your feelings can be exhausting but it can help you to make some sense of things.

Finn leaned over towards the mashed, broken, swollen body in the bed that he now knew was his best friend, and started to talk. He told Toad about how angry he'd been after his dad picked him up early from the party. He told him about having to talk at Mouth's funeral. He told him that he'd piked out of going to Church and Baz's funeral. He told him how everyone looked at him funny, like he should have died too and he told him how lonely he felt. Once he started to talk, everything just seemed to pour out. Weeks and weeks of being sad, scared, embarrassed, angry, frustrated and lonely all came rushing out of his mouth. When he finished he took a big breath and slumped back in the chair.

Finn sat there for a long time, just thinking. Thinking about the future. How will Toad play footy with one arm? Will girls still be interested in him? Will his face ever look normal again? Will he be able to walk properly? Will he remember all the stuff that happened before the accident? He finally stood up and leaned over towards the bed. He touched Toad gently on the shoulder, putting his hand over Mr Toad's head.

DON'T WORRY

When things change all of a sudden we can be scared of what the future holds because it's not the future we'd imagined.

'I'll come back in tomorrow, mate. Better get brewing up a power fart and stir this place up a bit, eh?' he said.

Finn walked around to the end of the bed and glanced back over his shoulder. The sounds of the beeping machine and the sucking machine didn't seem quite so scary now. He noticed the familiar freckles on Toad's nose and the curly black hair on his chest.

Toad's mum walked over and stood next to him.

'Will he be OK?' Finn asked.

'The doctors are turning off his breathing machine tonight, Finn,' she said softly. 'If he breathes on his own he'll be OK.'

'What if he doesn't?' Finn asked.

'We're not thinking about that,' she replied sadly.

It took Finn a moment, but he suddenly realised what she meant. He raced back over to the bed and leaned in close to Toad's ear, being careful to avoid the tubes.

'Listen, Toad: Church, Baz and Mouth are gone. You're my best friend. When they turn off that machine, you bloody well breathe, OK? No matter how hard it is. You're gonna breathe. One breath at a time. RIGHT?'

That night Finn couldn't eat his dinner. He tried to watch TV, but he couldn't concentrate. He tried to do some of his maths homework, but the numbers kept swirling around in his head and made no sense. He went down the backyard and started to chop some wood. He swung the axe as hard as he could and each time the blade hit the wood he muttered, 'BREATHE.' He swung and swung in a gentle rhythm, 'Breathe, breathe, breathe,' he repeated.

Q –WHAT CAN I DO TO HELP A FRIEND WHO'S GRIEVING?

A –THE DO'S & DON'TS – – – – – – – – – – – – – –

DO spend time with your friend.

DON'T avoid them because you don't know what to say.

DO tell them you can't imagine how they must be feeling.

DON'T tell them you know how they feel, 'cause you don't—you're not them!

DO let them cry if they want to.

DON'T try to cheer them up.

DO be yourself.

DON'T try to fix it.

WHAT DOES GRIEF MEAN? — — — — — — — — — —

Grief is the reaction we have to the loss of something or someone we value. It's a very real and personal experience. And we grieve differently for each person or thing because each situation is different: the relationship we have with a pet is not the same as the relationship we have with a friend or a parent. There is no normal way to grieve—we are all different people and our relationships are all different.

We don't only grieve when someone dies. We grieve when we lose anything that's important to us. We can grieve when our relationship to someone close to us changes; if they are hurt in an accident and won't be the same as they used to be, or if they suddenly dump us and start hanging out with someone else.

YOU'RE NOT ALONE
We can grieve when we get dropped by a girlfriend or boyfriend 'cause we feel rejected and the person isn't in your life any more.

Sometimes other people can expect us to grieve in a certain way because that's how they did it, and if we don't do it their way they may worry about us. We need to remember that no two people have the same grief experience and each grief experience we have will be different.

SAD MOMENT
'Mum said I wasn't grieving properly 'cause I didn't cry, but I didn't want to cry. I didn't want to do anything.'
Harry, 12

Grieving can be hard to understand. One minute you might feel sad and the next you might find yourself feeling angry or scared. There are no patterns to our feelings and no right or wrong way of grieving. The important thing to remember is that you will grieve in the way that's right for you. So if you find yourself crying a lot that's OK, but not all people cry and that's OK too.

When more than one person dies, our feelings can be even more complicated. You might find yourself comparing how you feel about each person who has died. You might wonder why the feelings you have for one person are different to those you feel for someone else. The reason these feelings are not the same is because your relationship with each person is different. When someone you love dies, you grieve for them because you won't see them again but you also grieve because your relationship with them has changed. You can't hang out with them any more, you can't ring them up or talk to them like you used to. Your world has changed forever because someone you love is gone.

REMEMBER

Some important things to remember:
- Everyone grieves differently.
- There is no right or wrong way to grieve.
- Grief does not happen in stages or steps. Feelings will come and go minute-by-minute, day-by-day. In a really short space of time you might feel sad, then angry, then scared, then happy as you remember the person you love.

CHAPTER 2

WATCHING SOMEONE YOU LOVE DIE — — — — — — — —

Josh had never seen a dead person before. He sat by his dad's bed all night watching him struggle to breathe. Every now and then it seemed that he'd stopped breathing and Josh would lean over and watch his chest. Early in the morning as he leaned over to watch again, he realised his dad's chest was completely still and that's how it stayed. He kept looking for a long time but nothing changed. He didn't want to call his stepmum, Kerrie, just yet. He just wanted to sit there by Dad on his own. He wondered if Dad's spirit had left his body. He looked around the room to see if there was part of Dad looking down on him, but he couldn't see anything unusual.

Josh sat back in the big armchair. He tucked his legs up and pulled Dad's old woollen blanket around himself. He thought about how quickly Dad had gone from just being sick to being asleep most of the time. It was only three weeks since Dad's birthday when the whole family had got together. His mum had come all the way from Fiji to the party. Josh thought that was a bit weird at the time, but when he asked Dad about it he said that she had come to say goodbye. If Dad was right that probably explained why Kerrie and Mum had spent so much time out on the deck talking.

> 'I didn't want anyone interrupting the time I could spend with Dad. I found myself getting cross when anyone else came into the room. Later I realised they wanted to spend time with him on their own too.'
> Ben, 17

Josh thought about how angry he had been when his mum first left and then how happy he was for Dad when he hooked up with Kerrie. Josh liked Kerrie, but she wasn't his mum. Sometimes he'd found himself feeling jealous of how much time Dad spent with her. That's why he'd wanted to sit with Dad during the night as often as he could. This was their special time together. It didn't matter if Dad was asleep 'cause when he woke up, he'd prop himself up on the pillows and chat to Josh about all sorts of things. They talked about stuff that happened when Josh was little. Dad talked to Josh about why his mum had left and now he finally understood that it was nothing to do with him. Dad told Josh about when he was a kid and the stuff he used to do with his mates. One night when Dad woke up he said, 'Has anyone told you what dying looks like, mate?'

Josh hadn't known what to say. 'Nope.'

'What do you think happens?' Dad asked.

'Dunno, Dad . . . guess you just go to sleep and don't wake up.'

Josh had only seen people die on telly and they either looked very glamorous or were covered in blood and gore 'cause they'd been murdered. He didn't even think he wanted to know what it was really like.

'Is it messy?' Josh asked.

DID YOU KNOW?
In real life almost nine in ten deaths are due to cancer, heart disease and other chronic illness. In 2007 only one in ten deaths in Australia was due to accidents. So, death happens very differently to how it's shown on television.

'Well, Josh, I just have to guess 'cause I haven't seen anyone die either, but I did see my mum after she died and she looked pretty peaceful, but then she was pretty old so I don't know if that changes things.'

Dad seemed to drift off again and Josh picked up his DS to keep playing.

'You scared, Josh?'

Josh looked up at Dad. 'A bit,' he said.

'Me too,' said Dad. 'I'm not scared of the dying stuff, I just don't want to leave you guys.'

Josh felt tears prickling behind his eyes. He stared down at his DS even though he wasn't really concentrating on it at all. He didn't want to look into Dad's eyes 'cause he knew he would see his own face reflected there.

'What's going to happen, Dad?' he said.

'I don't know, mate. All I know is that I won't be around much longer.'

WHAT CAN HELP
If someone who's dying wants to talk about it with us, we need to listen. By talking about dying together we can share our fears and worries and comfort each other.

17

'How, Dad? How do you know that? You might get better. You might live longer than me. Nobody knows. You DON'T know.' Josh couldn't control the tears. They rolled down his cheeks in great rivers and dripped onto his knees. Why did Dad have to talk like that?

'Come and sit here with me, Josh,' Dad said, patting the bed.

Josh got up from the chair and moved over to the bed. He sat carefully next to Dad.

'Mate, I know you don't want to talk about this, but I want you to know what'll happen. I don't want you getting a fright.'

That was the night Dad told Josh all about what dying would look like. From what he said, it was nothing like it was on telly. And Dad had been right. He'd told Josh about how he'd get sleepier and sleepier. How his body wasn't working like it used to. He warned Josh that he might get a bit restless, but the nurse had said that if this happened she could give him some medicine to stop it, but that would make him even sleepier. Dad also told Josh that when his breathing stopped and started, he would die pretty soon.

'I'm dying, Josh. Nothing works any more. It's all I can do to keep breathing. I just want to close my eyes for a while.'

That was the last time Dad had talked to Josh.

Kerrie and Josh had taken it in turns sitting with Dad the past few nights. Josh's little brother and sister had come in and out but didn't understand what was happening, so they'd get bored when Dad didn't talk to them. Kerrie would put the little kids to bed and sit with Dad for a bit so Josh could have a shower and watch a bit of telly and then he'd get himself comfy in the big armchair next to Dad's bed and Kerrie would go off to sleep for a while.

WHAT CAN HELP
It's very tiring for families caring for a dying person at home. When someone we know has a dying family member it can help if we offer to do some chores. Babysitting, shopping or cleaning can help take the pressure off them a bit.

Josh had been sitting with Dad for a couple of hours when he noticed that his breathing had changed. He seemed to breathe for a while and then he'd stop. Then he'd start again and stop. Josh had thought about going to wake up Kerrie, but decided that he'd let her sleep a little longer. Josh just sat by Dad's bed and talked to him. He told him about what was happening at school. He told him about the footy and when he ran out of things to say, he just sat and held Dad's cold hand. This had gone on for ages before Dad had finally stopped breathing and not started again.

Even when we are well prepared for someone to die it still comes as a shock when they finally stop breathing.

Josh cried. Not loud sobs, but the quiet crying that comes from deep inside. The crying that makes your shoulders quiver and your nose run. He stayed next to Dad until the birds started chirping and the daylight started to sneak in under the curtains. That's how Kerrie found him.

WHAT CAN HELP
Spending time with someone we love after they have died allows us to say goodbye in or own way and helps us understand that they are really dead. This time can be very important to the person left behind.

Q—ARE PEOPLE ABLE TO DIE AT HOME?

A

Whether or not a person can die at home depends on a number of things. If they have a terminal disease, they have some time to decide where they would like to die. Everybody is different. Some people want to die at home, in familiar surroundings with the people they love. Others choose to die in a hospice or palliative care unit where they feel more comfortable having health professionals look after them and their day-to-day care is provided by staff. But they are still able to have family and friends visit whenever they like. In fact, family are able to stay with the person overnight if they want to.

For people who choose to die at home, they too can be supported by health professionals who specialise in care of the dying. Nurses and doctors visit the person at home and help manage their pain and any other symptoms. They may even have a volunteer who comes to visit and sit with them so the family can have a break. The visiting staff are there to help the person and their family prepare for the death, but also to help them get the most out of each day of living.

WHAT CAN HELP?

If you want to get support from your local palliative care service, go to the palliative care website for your state (listed in the back of this book), type in your postcode, and the name and contact details for your local service will come up. Then just ring them and ask for help; OR go directly to the National Palliative Care Service Directory <http://pallcare.gky.com.au/c/pc?a-apps&ap-bd&sc-search> and fill in your postcode.

DO YOU KNOW WHAT DEATH LOOKS LIKE? — — — — —

There is always a first time for each of us to experience death. Our uncertainty about what dying looks like is reinforced by how it is shown on television, in the movies and in computer games. Death is not usually anything like this in real life.

People die for all sorts of reasons. In Western countries the most common causes of death are degenerative diseases that come with age, diseases that are caused by people's bodies wearing out. Heart disease, lung disease and cancer are the most common. Of course small numbers of people still die in accidents and in other unexpected ways. It's important to remember that people can die at any time throughout their lives, from childhood onwards, but it's more common in the older age groups.

> When a person is dying of a degenerative disease, this simply means that their body is wearing out from the disease.

When people die from diseases that cause their bodies to wear out, it usually happens slowly. They usually get sicker and sicker over time. They become less able to do the things they used to do when they were well. They lose weight and start to get tired after doing the smallest amount of exercise. They may start to get forgetful and sleepy, too.

Sometimes when someone is dying from a chronic disease they lose so much weight they look like a different person. This is because their body can't process food properly any more, so they don't build muscle or store fat. Over time, they may lose their appetite totally. This makes it hard for the people they love. The person dying doesn't feel like eating and the people around them sometimes try to entice them to eat so they'll get stronger. We need to remember that when someone is dying it doesn't matter what they do, the disease slowly takes its toll on their body.

The best thing we can do is to help them stay comfortable. Let them do what they want to do; sleep when they are tired, eat what they feel like eating (even if they only feel like ice cream) and spend their energy on the things that matter to them. The most important thing is to spend time with them, even if that just means sitting by their bed while they sleep.

When someone is in the last days or hours of their life, all of their body systems start to shut down. They are asleep most of the time because they don't have the energy to stay awake. Their skin gets sweaty and pale. Their hands and feet start to feel really cold because their heart isn't able to pump the blood around their body properly any more. Gradually their breathing becomes irregular. They may breathe a little and then stop. Then eventually they will stop breathing all together and within minutes their heart will stop beating too. This is how death looks.

? **DID YOU KNOW?**
When someone is unconscious they can still hear you, so it's important to talk to them as if they were awake and alert. It can comfort them to know someone they love is with them. ?

Even when we know someone we love is going to die, it never seems quite real. We hope that they'll wake up all of a sudden and everything will be OK. This is because we don't want them to die, so we hang on to the hope that they'll get better, or that they won't die just yet. It's always a shock when they die, even though we knew all along that they would.

CHAPTER 3

I COULD DIE TOO – – – – – – – – – – – – – – – –

Izzie never thought much about dying. Like everyone else she'd seen dead birds and dead animals on the road, but no one she knew had died and so she really had no reason to think about it much. When her best friend Mel's little sister Zoe died, it scared her. Zoe was only three. She didn't die of cot death or an accident or anything out of the ordinary. She got a cold and two days later she was dead. It happened so quickly. Zoe was a fit and healthy little kid and all of a sudden she was dead, and it scared Izzie.

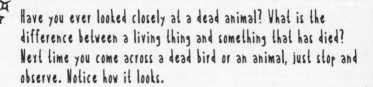

Have you ever looked closely at a dead animal? What is the difference between a living thing and something that has died? Next time you come across a dead bird or an animal, just stop and observe. Notice how it looks.

Izzie and Mel hung out together all the time. They went to school on the bus, played netball on the weekends and went to gigs in the city when they could con one of their parents to drive them. Izzie loved hanging out at Mel's place. Her mum and dad were great. They weren't up themselves like lots of other parents. They laughed and joked and listened to the same music that Izzie and Mel liked, but they weren't try-hard parents either. They were just really nice people.

Mel's house was always busy, 'cause she had two older brothers as well as her little sister, Zoe. Izzie loved talking to Mel's mum 'cause she got stuff that Izzie's mum just didn't get at all! She also made Izzie call her 'Jane', which Izzie thought was cool.

Zoe, Mel's little sister, was really cute. Whenever Izzie and Mel were sitting around talking, Zoe would come and cuddle them. They dressed her up in Mel's clothes and put make-up on her and crimped her hair. They taught her to sing Lily Allen songs (without the rude bits) and she'd dance around the lounge holding a hairbrush for a microphone, singing. When she got tired, she'd sit on the couch with them watching telly and doze off to sleep, lying across their laps.

This was all so different to Izzie's house. Izzie didn't have any brothers or sisters and her mum and dad worked long hours, so she was often home by herself and, though she hated to admit it, got lonely. She loved her mum and dad but they were always so busy. They were also a lot older than Mel's parents, and they had pretty old-fashioned ideas about things. That's why Izzie spent most of her free time at Mel's.

Izzie had never thought much about death. No one she knew had ever died. Of course, she saw stories on the news about people killed in accidents and famous people who died from drug overdoses or suicide, but she didn't know any of them so it didn't really bother her. Every now and then she'd wonder when her grandma or grandad would die, but they were pretty fit and healthy and she guessed they'd be around for a long time. Death didn't really figure much in her thoughts, until Zoe got sick.

WHAT CAN HELP
Today might be a good day to do something thoughtful for someone you love.

Izzie remembers that day well. She'd been over at Mel's playing Wii tennis when Zoe started sneezing. Jane put Zoe to bed and told Izzie and Mel to keep away from her because she had a temperature and she didn't want the girls catching it too. Izzie went home for dinner and didn't think too much about it. The next day at school Mel told Izzie that Zoe was really sick and her mum was taking her to the doctor. In the middle of the second last period, the secretary came into their class and spoke to their teacher.

'Mel, pack up your books, your dad's coming to pick you up,' she said. Mel packed up her books and whispered to Izzie, 'I'll call you from the car.' And with that she left the classroom.

Izzie waited and waited but Mel didn't call. She texted her but didn't get an answer. When school finished she rang Mel's mobile again, but it just went to her message bank. Izzie started to worry. Mel never ignored a call from Izzie unless she was angry about something, but that didn't happen very often.

SAD MOMENT
'The worst part was that no one told me what was going on. I knew something was wrong, but no one would talk about it.'
Karen, 9

On the way home Izzie walked past Mel's house but there were no cars in the drive, and when she knocked on the door there was no answer. When Izzie got back to her place she went online and checked to see if Mel was on Facebook, but she hadn't put a comment on her page either. So Izzie did her homework and watched TV till her Mum came in from work.

'How come you're home so early, Iz? Didn't you go to Mel's tonight?' her mum asked as she dumped the shopping on the bench.

Izzie told her what had happened at school.

'I'll call Jane and see what's happening if you like?'

'No, Mum, she's probably still at the doctor's or maybe they've had to take Zoe to hospital. Mel will call when she gets home.'

But Mel didn't call that night. In fact, she didn't call the next day and she didn't turn up to school either. Izzie began to get scared. What the hell could be going on? That night while she was having dinner with her mum and dad, Izzie took a deep breath and asked the question that was worrying her.

'Mum, you don't think anything bad has happened to Zoe, do ya?'

'Surely not, Iz, she's a healthy little kid. She's probably just got an infection or something. That swine flu thing has been going around and little ones are more susceptible than adults. Maybe it's that,' Mum said.

'But people die from that,' said Izzie anxiously.

'Only old or sick people, Izzie. But it is contagious, so maybe they've put her in hospital so she doesn't spread it around,' chimed in her dad.

Izzie felt a bit relieved; maybe Mum and Dad were right and she was overreacting. Just as she began to relax, the phone rang. Izzie flew out of her chair and ran over to the bench, but before she could pick up the handset her mum said, 'I'll get it, Iz.'

Izzie knew by the look on Mum's face as soon as she picked up the phone that something bad had happened.

'Oh Jane,' was all she said.

Mum turned her back to the wall so Izzie couldn't see her face. When she hung up, she walked straight over to Izzie and put her arm around her.

That had all happened hours ago. Now Izzie was lying in her bed staring at the ceiling, replaying in her head the conversation she'd had with her mum and dad, the phone ringing and her mum telling her that Zoe had just died in the hospital. Izzie had wanted to ring Mel, but her mum said not to bother her right now.

DON'T WORRY
When someone young dies, we often think it's not fair 'cause they have not had a long life. But it doesn't matter how old or young someone is, the people who love them will always grieve for them whether they're nine months old or ninety-nine years old.

'Jane said Mel will ring you tomorrow, Iz, just leave it at that.' But Izzie couldn't. Her mind was racing. How could Zoe be dead? She's only a baby. Why didn't some old person die instead? This just isn't fair.

Then she began to think about how Zoe must look in her hospital bed, all cold and still. She wondered if her eyes were open and staring into space or if they were closed and she just looked like she did when she slept on the couch with her and Mel. Izzie wondered if the nurses would put her straight into a coffin and take her away. Where would they put her? Would Mel's family have to take the coffin home? Then Izzie wondered if they made little coffins for kids or whether they just put her in a big one. The thoughts kept rattling round and round in her head.

DON'T WORRY

When someone dies unexpectedly it is normal to try and imagine how they must look, especially if when we saw them last they were happy and healthy. This is just our mind trying to understand that they have died.

All the time she was thinking these weird things, she couldn't stop crying. She loved Zoe. She was like her own little sister. The sister she'd never get. She thought about Mel and Jane. She thought about Mel's brothers and her dad and wondered if they were crying too. Izzie had never seen a man cry.

Then some really scary thoughts started to pop into her head. If a fit and healthy kid like Zoe could die from a cold that turned into something called 'pneumonia', it could happen to anyone. It could happen to Mum or Dad. It could happen to Mel OR it could happen to Izzie herself! A sudden terrifying thought jumped into Izzie's mind. 'Mel and I were playing with Zoe. What if we've already got it and we don't know?'

SAD MOMENT

'When Dad died of a heart attack, I kept getting pains in my chest. I thought I was dying too, but the doctor said that was my body reacting to the pain I felt because he was dead.'
Aiden, 15

Izzie put her hand on her forehead and was sure it felt hot. Her throat felt dry. She had a headache. Her eyes were red and sore. Was it just because she'd been crying or was she about to get really sick, too?

Q—WHY IS THINKING ABOUT DYING SO SCARY?

A————————————————————

Whether we think about it or not, we are going to die eventually. Thinking about dying helps us to confront our fears and make sense of them. If we try to ignore our fears we allow them to have more power over us. If we are scared of dying we are tempted to avoid doing lots of things that we think might cause our death, like swimming, crossing the road or learning to drive. By exploring our fears, talking to people we trust and making sense of death we allow ourself to truly live our life, with all its joys and sorrows.

WHAT CAN HELP
Some questions you might want to think about:
- What bits about dying are you scared of?
- Have you ever talked to your family about death?
- How could you start a conversation with them?
- Do you have someone you can talk to about your fears?

THINKING ABOUT OUR OWN DEATH — — — — — — —

We all think of ourselves as being immortal. Even though we know in our hearts that one day we'll die, we always think of our death as being far off in the future. It doesn't matter how young or old we are, we don't think about our own death very often.

No one ever thinks when they get up in the morning, *Today is the day I'll die*, but for some people it is. On any day around the world, millions of people who didn't expect to die, do.

When someone close to us dies it calls into question all that we previously knew as certain. It makes us question our own mortality and therefore our own fears about dying and about what happens after we die. This can be scary.

We start to wonder about how we'll die. *Will I die suddenly in an accident or get a disease and die slowly?* When we think about how we'll die, it brings up a whole lot of questions. It makes us think about things we may not have had a chance to do. It makes us think about the future we have planned in our mind and whether we'll get a chance to live the life we've imagined. It makes us think about things we may regret, people we may have been unkind to, arguments we may have had with people we love.

We always think we'll have plenty of time to make up for mean things we've done but when someone close dies, we start to question whether we *do* have time. It may not seem like it, but this is actually a healthy process.

33

Thinking about our life up till now gives us an opportunity to change things we feel bad about. It also allows us to refocus on the things that are the most important to us, the people we care about and the world we live in. It helps us to concentrate on living every minute of every day. On seeing the beauty in the world around us, on being grateful for the life we have, for the friends, the family and the things we value. It also helps us to see the injustices in the world. To look beyond our own experiences and see how other people live. This is often an opportunity to think about what we can do to make the world a better place. It helps us to look outside ourself.

So, when someone close to us dies, not only are we trying to make sense of the pain we feel because they're gone, but we are trying to understand our own feelings about dying. This time is important: it can be a turning point in our life. This time gives us an opportunity to get to know ourself, to understand our thoughts and feelings and to plan how we want to live the rest of our life.

CHAPTER 4

LIVING IN A NIGHTMARE — — — — — — — — — — —

Sarah couldn't eat. Her eyes were so red and puffy from crying, she could hardly see. She felt like a ghost, floating around, invisible. All she wanted was to climb into bed, wrapped in Mum's old dressing gown, go to sleep and never wake up, 'cause when she was asleep everything went back to normal. She forgot Mum was dead.

DON'T WORRY
When you think about the fun times you had with the person you love before they died, it will hurt because you miss them. But these memories also remind you of what you shared so they can make you feel happy, too.

Though she wouldn't admit it, 'cause that's not cool, Sarah felt sooo alone. Mum was more like a friend than a mother; she could tell her everything. But now she was gone, who could she talk to? Sarah's friends were great, but no one understood. They didn't get the relationship Sarah had with her mum, because they were bossed around and treated like idiots by their own mums. None of Sarah's friends got why she and Mum went to concerts or why Sarah looked forward to going shopping together. They would go to all the coolest shops, then have lunch at a funky cafe and make up stories about the people walking past. The stories became crazier and ruder the longer they sat there. But that was then; now the memories were all she had left and it made her feel empty inside.

DID YOU KNOW?

Grief has an impact on our whole self. In the first days and weeks after someone we love dies people often feel that nothing is real. You may sometimes feel like you're walking around in a daze. You can't think clearly. And you may feel sad, withdrawn and angry all at once.

Sarah thought about the day, not long ago, when she had arrived home from school early to find Mum curled up on the couch crying. Mum only cried when something terrible happened. Sarah had dropped her bag on the floor and sat next to Mum. 'Mum, what's wrong?' she asked, scared of what the answer might be. Mum had thrown her arms around Sarah and said, 'I'm so sorry, Sez.' She died six weeks later.

Everything that had happened since then seemed to be a blur. Sarah remembered bits of the whispered discussions Mum had with her friends when they came to visit. She remembered the disgusting sound of Mum chucking up in the bathroom. She also remembered how awful Mum looked as she got skinnier and skinnier. Worst of all she remembered the look on Dad's face as he sat holding Mum's hand and telling her it would be all right, when they both knew he was lying.

Now her Mum was dead. Sarah couldn't remember what day it was. Sometimes it seemed like weeks since Mum died. At other times she expected to see Mum in the kitchen, sitting in the lounge watching TV or taking the washing up the stairs. It was all too hard.

WHAT CAN HELP
Sometimes people think that talking about what's happening in their own life can distract the grieving person for a while and make them feel better. But this usually just makes the grieving person feel more alone because their world is not normal any more. They feel like they are living in a nightmare and can't wake up.

A friend who's grieving doesn't want you to fix it for them, 'cause they know you can't. All they want is someone to listen and BE with them.

Sarah's head hurt. She had a pain in her guts that wouldn't go away. It made her feel sick. Her bones ached. Her brain felt like it was clouded in fog. She couldn't think straight. She wanted to yell and scream, even to hit someone. She hated her friends, who kept bitching about unimportant things like who copied someone's hair, or who pashed whose boyfriend on the weekend. She just wanted to scream, 'I don't give a shit, my mum's DEAD.' But she didn't.

DON'T WORRY
Everyone grieves differently and sometimes it can be hard to understand why other people are doing things that seem weird to you.

That's why she didn't answer the phone any more. And when they came to visit, she told them to go away. She did what she had to do. She got her clothes ready for the funeral, nodded politely at the continuous stream of relatives who kept arriving at the house, but didn't talk to anyone much. There just weren't any words for how she was feeling. She collected a whole heap of photos of Mum. Dad had asked her to put them together in an album, but she didn't understand why he wanted this done right now.

As soon as she could get away she'd sneak upstairs to her room, get Mum's old dressing gown from where she'd hidden it, wrap herself up in its fluffy folds and curl up on her bed. This was the only place in the whole world she felt safe. Here she could cry till she ran out of tears, then sleep, hoping that when she woke up it would all be just a bad dream.

WHAT CAN HELP

Cuddling up to things that are familiar, that smell or feel like the person who has died can help the grieving person to feel safe.

Sarah snuggled against the folds of the dressing gown, running her fingers along the worn embroidery on the pocket, then closed her eyes and thought about Mum. She imagined them sitting together drinking peppermint tea in a little street cafe. As she drifted off to sleep, she thought she could feel her mum's arms around her. Then Sarah heard Mum whisper softly, 'Look at that skanky blonde woman over there, Sez, she thinks she's Paris Hilton . . . she even has a little dog in her D&G bag!' Then as the picture in her mind faded Sarah drifted off into a deep, deep sleep for the first time in ages.

Q–AM I JUST IMAGINING THIS PAIN?

A

It's important to remember that the physical symptoms we experience in the first days and weeks after the death of someone close are very real. These symptoms are the body's attempt to help us cope after the death. Listen to your body. If you don't feel hungry don't force yourself to eat a big meal, maybe snack on some fruit and vegetables. Remember to drink plenty of water and to sleep when you feel tired. Always talk to an adult you trust if you have distressing physical symptoms. You may be feeling sick because you have an infection or an illness that is nothing to do with the death. It is always wise to see a health professional if you are worried.

WHAT HELPED ME
'I couldn't face a big dinner for weeks after Dad died. All I wanted to eat was fruit salad, so I did.'
Bobo, 14

WHY DO I FEEL SO CRAP? — — — — — — — — — —

The first days and weeks after someone we love dies can seem like a bad dream. We may feel like we imagined the death, and that if we just concentrate really hard things will go back to normal. You might feel that you are not in the same space that your friends are in. You may feel totally isolated and alone. Things that were important, like hanging out with mates, looking good, being popular or winning at sport, don't seem so important.

SAD MOMENT

'I remember feeling like I was totally on my own. Like no one else got it.'
Gaby, 14

'I remember feeling sick all the time and thinking that was awful, until a couple of weeks later I started to feel sad and it never went away.'
Stig, 16

'My worst day was when my aunty started cleaning out Mum's wardrobe. She had no right. Those are Mum's things. Leave them alone!'
Jason, 17

The death of someone we love is always a shock, even when we know the person is going to die. Sometimes people think it's easier if the death is expected, but a death is still a death. Whether you know beforehand or not doesn't make it hurt any less. Watching someone you love slowly deteriorate over weeks or months can be extremely distressing. When someone dies unexpectedly, it is often hard to believe the person you loved is really dead.

REMEMBER

If you are having scary feelings or imagine hurting yourself, talk to someone you trust. You can always call Kids Helpline: 1800 55 1800, or Lifeline: 13 11 14.

In the first few days and weeks after the person you love has died, you may go into a form of shock. This shock may impact on you in a number of ways. Apart from the feelings of sadness, distress or anger, you may have strange thoughts and find yourself thinking about what their body will look like when it starts to decay in the ground, or you may think that life is too hard and you just want to lie down and die too.

WILL LIFE EVER GET BETTER?

'It started slowly. A minute here. A minute there. One day I realised I actually felt happy.'
Sam, 16

You may find yourself thinking about why the person died and start to blame yourself; we talk more about this in Chapter 6. You can also have very physical reactions. It is common in the first days after the death to not want to eat because you don't feel hungry. You may feel sick, or even vomit. You may have headaches, pains in the belly or aching bones. You might even have a severe pain that is similar to the pain experienced by the person who died. Why does this happen?

The shock of the death causes our body to release hormones and other chemicals to help us cope with stress, to numb our emotional pain. Our body's reactions in the early days after the death of someone we love are like the responses we'd have if we had to sit an exam that our whole future depended on but which we hadn't done any study for. Nausea, sweating, feeling constantly thirsty, racing heart, butterflies in the gut, not being able to sit still, or simply wanting to find any way of escape are all common physical responses to our body being flooded with these survival chemicals.

DID YOU KNOW?
The tears you cry when you are grieving are different from the tears you get any other time, because they contain special chemicals that make you feel numb.

In these early days of grieving special chemicals are released in our tears that stop us thinking clearly and create the foggy brain that people often talk about. These chemicals, the body's natural narcotics, have the same sort of impact as morphine or other strong pain-relieving drugs and that's their purpose—to help relieve the pain of grief. This is why crying can often make us feel better, for a little while at least.

As the days go by and the initial shock of the death passes, we begin to understand that the person really has died and is not coming back in a physical sense. That's when our pain can become less physical; now our deep feelings and thoughts start to occupy more of our attention.

WHAT HELPED ME
'Some things that really helped me in the first few days were:
- having time to myself;
- being able to cry when I needed to;
- being surrounded by people who were sad too.'
Mario, 13

CHAPTER 5

AM I GOING CRAZY? – – – – – – – – – – – – –

Luke was confused. He knew his best friend, Eddie, was dead. He heard the scream of the brakes and saw him get hit by the car. He saw him being put into the ambulance and the flashing lights. He went to the funeral and saw the coffin lowered into the ground, yet he found himself chasing after Eddie in his dreams. He thought he saw him at the supermarket next to the frozen foods. He was sure he heard Eddie calling him while he was playing footy. What the hell was going on? Was he going nuts?

> **DON'T WORRY**
> When we are comfortable and safe, drifting off to sleep, our subconscious mind allows all the thoughts we've been avoiding during the day to come to life.

Every night when Luke got into bed he thought to himself, *I won't think about Eddie tonight and then I won't dream about him*. But every time he cuddled down under his doona and closed his eyes, it was like a DVD was pulled out of a cupboard in his brain and the movie of the day Eddie was killed played again in his head. It always started the same way.

They were on their way home from the skate park. They'd just met up with Beck and Gabby, the two hottest chicks at school. Luckily Eddie had a thing for Beck and Luke for Gabby, so there was no hassle about who'd get who. They just had to impress both girls enough and finally they'd have girlfriends—and they'd done pretty well so far. It had been a great day.

Eddie was on fire! He was a gun skater and managed to impress Beck by pulling off an ollie from the top of the half pipe. She even hugged him afterwards and told him he should be a professional. Luke won over Gabby in his own way by majorly stacking and taking all the skin off his elbow. Gabby came running. 'Luke, you OK?' she asked anxiously.

'Yeah, I'm OK. It hurts like crap though.'

Luke had to admit, he pretended it was a whole lot worse than it really was. He didn't care if he got the sympathy vote so long as he got Gabby. She pulled a packet of make-up remover wipes from her bag and wiped the blood from his arm, which was red raw. Luke didn't feel a thing; he just looked at her as she gently dabbed at his arm. *Jeez, she's cute*, he thought.

'Stop gawking at me,' she said, but she wasn't angry. She looked him straight in the eyes and smiled.

Of course Eddie had to interrupt right when he thought Gabby might give him a kiss.

'Poor little Lukie,' he said in a girlie voice as he skated over to where Luke was still sitting on the ground.

'Shut up, Eddie, he's hurt,' said Gabby.

'I'm fine,' said Luke as he stood up. He wasn't really, but he didn't want Gabby to think he was a pussy. 'But thanks, Gabby, it feels much better now,' he added.

Gabby smiled again.

'I have to go. Walk me down the road, Luke?' Gabby asked.

'Sure,' he said.

'I gotta go too,' said Beck, looking at Eddie.

'I'll walk ya,' replied Eddie.

As they all headed out of the skate park together, Eddie whispered to Luke: 'We're in, mate. Meet you at your corner when you've dropped her off.'

'Don't know how long I'll be,' Luke whispered back.

'Whoever gets there first waits, right?'

'OK,' Luke said as he moved over towards Gabby.

Luke and Gabby headed towards the shops and Eddie and Beck went in the opposite direction. Luke looked back over his shoulder and saw Eddie put his arm around Beck. *Damn*, he thought, *I have to do something or Eddie will give me crap.* So, before he had a chance to feel nervous, he grabbed for Gabby's hand. Strangely it wasn't hard at all. As soon as he reached his hand out, she grabbed it and squeezed. They walked along for a bit, just holding hands and not saying anything. Gabby leaned in towards Luke and put her head on his shoulder.

'How's the elbow feel?' she asked.

'Pretty bloody sore,' Luke said. But to be honest it felt totally numb. He was more worried about his heart, which was beating so fast he was scared to talk in case it jumped clean out of his mouth and landed splat on the footpath.

Before Luke had a chance to ask Gabby to go with him, he looked up and noticed they were just up the road from her house. Gabby dropped his hand.

'What's up?' he asked.

'Mum would spew. See you tomorrow?'

'Sure. Down the park?'

'At school, you idiot,' she said, and they both laughed.

Luke couldn't think. His heart was still going bonkers and his throat felt so dry he could hardly talk.

'OK, meet you at the shops? We could walk together.'

'What about Eddie?' Gabby asked, 'cause she knew Luke and Eddie always skated to school together.

'Oh bugger Eddie,' laughed Luke.

Gabby began to walk down her driveway. She turned back and called out, 'OK, outside the butcher's at eight?'

Luke dropped his skater onto the ground, smiled towards Gabby and gave her the thumbs up.

'Eight!' he called back as he jumped onto his skater and headed down the middle of the road. He wanted to jump up and down . . . he was IN! Gabby liked him and he liked her. Perfect. He couldn't wait to tell Eddie.

As Luke rounded the corner he saw Eddie skating down the middle of the road about 600 metres away. Eddie was heading towards his favourite roundabout. He'd recently mastered his best trick yet. He'd skate flat stick to the roundabout, and when he reached the curb on the edge he'd jump so high he'd clear the whole roundabout, land on the road on the other side and just keep on skating. Amazing! Luke didn't even bother trying 'cause he knew he wasn't in the same league. Luke put his head down and pushed his foot down hard and fast on the road so he could speed up and reach the roundabout in time to see Eddie do his jump.

He heard the noise before he saw anything. A car was belting round the corner, past him, heading for the roundabout.

REMEMBER

Sometimes we think we are invincible. We don't stop and consider the risks of dangerous behaviour. We need to remind ourselves that it's not always about our abilities. We can't predict the behaviour of others.

'EDDIE,' he yelled.

Eddie didn't hear Luke—he was so focused on getting up enough speed to make the jump—and he didn't see the car.

'EDDIE, OH SHIT . . . EDDIE!' Luke screamed. He put his head down and skated as fast as he could but he didn't seem to be moving. He seemed to get no closer.

DID YOU KNOW?

Knowing instantly that something terrible is going to happen starts our heart racing, dilates our pupils, pumps blood to our muscles and gets us ready to run or fight.

Luke heard the scream of the brakes first, then a deafening thud and the crunch of metal as the car bounced over the roundabout and crashed into the brick fence in front of the child care centre. Luke could smell burning rubber and the smoke that was pouring out of the car. He dumped his skateboard and started to run towards the roundabout. He saw a lady running towards him. 'STOP!' she yelled, but he kept running, he was almost there.

'STOP!' he heard again as the lady reached him and grabbed his arm, 'Stop, love, don't go up there.'

'Let me go! He's my best friend.'

Luke shook her off but when he got to the edge of the roundabout he stopped. He couldn't move. He just stood there looking, searching for some sign of Eddie. He couldn't see him anywhere. Then he noticed his skateboard lying on the side of the road snapped in half.

Luke walked slowly towards the car that was making an awful hissing sound as water poured out of the engine. He saw a man in the driver's seat, slumped over the steering wheel. All he could smell was oil and petrol and smoke.

SAD MOMENT
'I froze. The world seemed to have stopped. It was like I was watching everything in slow motion.'
Cooper, 14

'For Christ's sake, someone get an ambulance,' he yelled to the people who were now rushing out of their houses. The lady who had tried to stop him before was beside him now. 'Please, love, stay here, an ambulance and the police are on their way.'

'Eddie's in there somewhere,' he said. 'I've gotta find him.'

DID YOU KNOW?
Sometimes our brain tries to save us from the trauma by burying the worst images so deep that we have trouble picturing them afterwards.

'He's under the car . . .' But before she could finish, Luke dropped to his knees and was trying to move in under the smoking, twisted pile of metal. If he could only get under there he could get Eddie out.

And that's when he always wakes up screaming and sweating, his heart beating like it is about to break through his chest. It's always the same, he can never see Eddie in his dreams or when he is awake and trying to remember. His memory always stops at the point where he began to crawl underneath the car. The frustrating thing is he KNOWS he found Eddie because he tried to pull him out, but he was stuck. He knows he saw Eddie's face, but he can't remember it no matter how hard he tries. He remembers nothing more until the next day.

WHAT HELPED ME
'People not asking questions. I couldn't remember. I didn't want to remember. I didn't want people asking me stuff.'
Nick, 15

The next day the weird stuff started to happen. He thought he saw Eddie off in the distance when he went for a walk to get out of the house, but when he chased after him Eddie just disappeared. A couple of days later, he thought he saw Eddie at the cemetery standing at the edge of the crowd as they lowered his coffin into the ground. He thought he saw Eddie at school during lunchtime standing under one of the big trees by the footy oval, but when he ran over there Eddie was gone.

'What the hell are you doing, Eddie,' he screamed as he slumped down onto the ground under the tree.

DID YOU KNOW?

When we witness something traumatic, all the sights, smells, sounds, feelings and tastes of that moment are imprinted in our brain. Whenever we see, hear, feel, taste or smell something similar, we are immediately transported back to the incident as if it was happening all over again. Over time we can learn to predict some of the things that are likely to transport us back to the traumatic incident. Learning some relaxation and breathing exercises can help us to cope with these flashbacks when they happen.

Luke put his head on his knees, wanting to cry but not wanting anyone to see him. He couldn't bear the sound of kids playing. He couldn't stand the smell of petrol or smoke. Every time he heard a car brake he felt the bitter taste of vomit rise in the back of his throat. He knew all these things took him back to the day Eddie was killed and yet he still couldn't remember what Eddie looked like under that bloody car. He tried and tried to see Eddie's face, but he just couldn't. He just kept seeing him as he used to look, popping up in all the places where they used to hang out together.

Q–WHO CAN HELP ME?

A

There is plenty of help available if you've had a traumatic grief experience. But if you don't want to go to someone's office, there are lots of internet support services and telephone help lines listed in the back of this book. The most important thing to remember is to ask for help. People who care about you are often scared of interfering in case it makes things worse for you.

Always talk to people you feel comfortable with. What you are experiencing is perfectly normal for you, so you don't need to feel scared or ashamed to talk about your thoughts and feelings no matter how weird you might think they are.

As a friend, the best support you can give to someone grieving is to spend time with them. Don't try to distract them or avoid the subject, just be your normal self. If your friend wants to talk about the death they will, but don't force them. Just being there for them is all you need to do.

☺ **BEST MOMENT**
'When I went back to school there was a bunch of flowers on my locker. I don't know who put them there. I cried 'cause I felt like someone understood.'
Olivia, 17 ☺

WHEN EVERYTHING JUST STOPS — — — — — — — — —

When we face danger, time appears to stop. Our nervous system that controls our brain, our nerves and the movement of our muscles produces chemicals that can give us extra human strength and slow our thinking so we're able to focus on the immediate danger. Our heart rate increases and extra blood is pumped to our muscles. Our breathing speeds up and we may have tunnel vision (so that we are only seeing what is directly in front of us) and we'll sweat and feel agitated. These reactions are called the fight-or-flight response.

Whenever we are in a situation where we feel under threat, the fight-or-flight response is activated. You'd notice this happening if something suddenly frightens you.

The fight-or-flight response kicks in not just when you feel under threat, but also when you witness someone else in danger. The world seems to stand still, time slows down and your whole focus is on getting to safety. After the danger has passed, memories of the incident can be confused. You might remember small things in minute detail and other aspects of the event as a blur. Often the most traumatic elements are hard to remember. This is your brain's way of trying to protect you from the emotional pain of the experience.

When a traumatic event, like witnessing an accident, is combined with the death of someone close, the combination of the trauma and the grief can make strange things happen. Dreaming over and over again about the incident, but the dreams stop before the end. Waking dreams where you think you see the person in the normal places where they hung out before they died. Hearing the voice of the person who died talking to you. You might also find yourself reliving the event when you see, hear or smell things that act as a trigger, taking you back to the moment of the accident.

WHAT HELPED ME
'After a while I actually looked forward to hearing her voice. I knew it wasn't really Mum, it was just a memory, but it felt nice.'
Tom, 14

All of this can be really upsetting but is normal for someone who has experienced trauma. The important thing to remember is to ask for help. No one needs to try and make sense of these experiences on their own. There are lots of people who can help: counsellors, trusted friends and support groups. Talking to other people who have had traumatic experiences helps us to understand that we are not alone.

CHAPTER 6

IT'S ALL MY FAULT! — — — — — — — — — — — — — —

Kassie felt so alone. Her mum and dad didn't talk to her. Every time she walked into the room they'd stop speaking.

They blame me, she thought. *If I hadn't thought all those awful things about her, I'd still have my little sister. It's all my fault!*

Kassie's little sister, Elise, was born twelve weeks before she should have been. Kassie remembered the first time she saw her in the hospital. Elise was lying in a big glass box, and she had tubes going into her little arms and legs and a tube in her nose. She was all wrinkly, like she'd spent too long in the bath. She had jaundice, Mum explained, which was why her skin was a dark orange colour. She had a mesh patch covering her eyes, a tiny little knitted hat on her head and a nappy that looked like it was made for a doll, but apart from that she was naked under the big floodlights that kept her warm. Kassie couldn't believe how tiny she was. In fact, she really didn't look like a baby at all, she looked more like one of those orange baby monkeys that you see at the zoo but not quite as hairy.

Kassie had been so excited about having a little sister. Mum and Dad had told her months before she was born that the baby was going to be a girl. Kassie had spent lots of her spare time making things for her little sister's room. She'd painted pictures for the wall. She'd made little figures out of felt that Mum had strung into a mobile to hang over the top of the baby's change table. She'd helped Mum sand the old cot and repaint it.

Kassie's friends were all excited, too. None of them had baby brothers or sisters. Even though they all thought it was gross that Kassie's mum and dad were still doing it, they were all looking forward to playing around with the baby when it was born. But it hadn't turned out how they'd all expected.

The day Kassie's mum went into labour Kassie was at school in the middle of an exam, so she didn't find out until she got home and Gran was there.

'Mum's gone into labour, Kass,' said Gran, as she came in the back door.

'But it's too soon,' said Kassie. 'Will she be OK?'

'I'm sure she will,' said Gran, who kept on cutting up vegetables at the kitchen table.

'When can I go and see her?' Kassie asked as she dropped her bag by the fridge and gave her gran a kiss.

'We just have to wait till we hear from your dad,' said Gran.

They didn't hear anything from the hospital till late that night. Gran had made Kassie go to bed but promised that if Dad rang, she'd wake her straight away. It was about two in the morning when Kassie heard Gran's voice. 'Kassie, love, Kassie.'

'Is the baby born?' asked Kassie, rubbing her eyes and trying to wake herself up.

Gran sat on the bed next to Kassie and stroked her silky, brown hair away from her eyes. 'Yes, Kass, the baby's born.'

Kassie looked at Gran. She had aged a lot in the last year. Something about the look in her eyes made Kassie sit up.

'What's up, Gran? Is everything OK?'

'Kassie, the baby is very small. She has a fight on her hands.'

'Is Mum OK?'

'Your mum's fine, but she's exhausted. It's been a long, tiring business and now the real hard work will start. The baby will need a lot of care.'

'I want to see her,' Kassie said. She tried to get out of bed.

'Not tonight, lovey. I'll take you to the hospital in the morning. Your dad will be home by then.'

DID YOU KNOW?

When a new baby arrives it can sometimes make other kids in the family question things. Because the baby needs so much attention, other kids can feel forgotten.

That first visit Kassie made to the hospital with Gran and Dad was just the beginning of weeks of hospital visits.

It got to the point where Kassie felt she may as well just live at the hospital. Mum had come home three days after Elise was born, but Elise had to stay until she was big enough to manage outside the glass box. Kassie hardly saw her mum and dad, except when she visited the hospital every day after school. There they'd be, in the same place, one on either side of the glass box with their arms in the inside-out gloves that allowed them to touch Elise without giving her germs. They would look up and smile and then turn back to the glass box and stare at the little orange monkey baby that was Kassie's little sister.

Kassie began to feel angry. She felt like her mum and dad had deserted her. She stopped going to the hospital every night and they didn't even notice. They were never home, they never spoke to her. Dad left for work before Kassie got up and didn't come home till late at night after leaving the hospital. Mum was still in bed every morning when Kassie left for school. When Mum came home late each night with Dad she looked exhausted and went straight to bed. Even Gran couldn't talk about anything except the baby. She tried hard to interest Kassie in the latest news about her little sister.

'Elise has put on .05 of a gram, Kass. Isn't that great?'

'Yeah, great,' said Kassie. She stormed out of the kitchen and up to her room.

Gran was just trying to help. Kassie knew that but she was sick of hearing about the number of poos Elise had yesterday or how she was drinking an extra 10 millilitres of milk. The orange monkey baby seemed to be all anyone cared about or could talk about and she'd had enough. *I just wanted a little sister who I could play with and cuddle, not some freak in a glass box that everyone talks about non stop*, she thought while she lay on her bed looking at the ceiling.

SAD MOMENT
'When I realised that the plan I'd made in my head was NOT how it was going to be.'
Hannah, 12

One night when Mum and Dad came in from the hospital, Kassie said, 'Mum, I need to get a dress for the school formal. Can we go shopping on Saturday?'

'Not now, Kass, I'm too tired to think about it.'

'But, Mum, the formal's only three weeks away.'

'NOT NOW, I said. I've got more important things to worry about,' said Mum as she flopped down on the couch and kicked off her shoes.

SAD MOMENT
'I just wanted someone to notice me. I felt left out, like Mum and Dad were so worried, but they couldn't tell me about it. I wish they'd told me Nanna was dying.'
James, 14

'What more important things? How many poos monkey baby's had today?' snapped Kassie as she pushed past her dad and stormed out of the room. She ran to her bedroom and threw herself onto the bed, buried her head in the pillow and punched it hard with both her fists. There was a knock on the door.

'Can I come in, Kass?' asked her dad.

'Go away!' yelled Kassie.

She heard the door open and felt her father's hand on her back.

'We need to talk, Kassie,' he said.

Kassie rolled over and looked at her dad. He looked tired. He had big, black circles under his eyes and he needed a haircut. He sat on the edge of her bed.

'You need to go a bit easy on Mum, love, she's under a lot of pressure,' he said gently.

REMEMBER
Sometimes when we're distressed it's hard to think about other people's feelings. When someone is dying or has died, everyone responds differently and it's helpful to remember that others won't grieve the same way as you.

'What about me, Dad? No one talks to me any more and when they do it's always about the baby. I'm sick of it. I may as well be dead. All anyone cares about is that monkey baby.'

'Please don't say that, Kass. Elise is very sick. She's losing weight and now she has an infection,' sighed Dad.

'I don't care. I could have died weeks ago and no one would have noticed. Even Gran can only talk about the bloody baby. I'm over it!'

Dad put his arms around Kassie and hugged her tight.

'I'm sorry, Kassie. I didn't realise. I'm so sorry,' Dad said softly. He patted her on the head and quietly got up and left the room.

REMEMBER
We can become so bound up in what we are feeling we forget to notice others.

That's right, thought Kassie. *Just forget about me.*

Two days later when Kassie came home from school she was surprised to see Dad's car in the driveway. *That's weird*, she thought. He mustn't have gone to the hospital. When Kassie walked in the back door, she immediately knew something was wrong. Mum was sitting at the kitchen table with her head in her hands, sobbing, and Dad was standing behind her rubbing her back. Gran was standing by the sink. She had tears dripping down her chin as she looked up at Kassie.

'What's going on?' asked Kassie.

WHAT CAN HELP
When people you care about are grieving, they may say things they don't mean because they can't think clearly and are so consumed by sadness. This doesn't mean they don't love you. The best way to deal with this is to take a deep breath, relax and leave the room for a while. This gives the person a chance to calm down.

Her mum looked up. She seemed to stare straight past Kassie into space, then she put her head back in her hands and whispered, 'Just get out of here.'

Gran walked over to Kassie and put her arm around her.

'Go into the lounge, Kass, I'll be there in a minute.'

Kassie waited in the lounge room for ages. She put the television on and tried to think what could be wrong. Obviously monkey baby must not have put on weight or maybe her mum has just lost it after weeks of living at the hospital. Gran came in and sat beside Kassie.

'There's no gentle way to tell you this, Kassie. Elise died this afternoon.'

'Wh . . . what?' stuttered Kassie. 'How could she die? I thought she'd put on weight and was coming home soon?'

'She got an infection,' Gran said. 'She just wasn't strong enough to fight it off.'

DON'T WORRY

When we've planned a future in our head and the person dies we don't only grieve for the fact that they've died, but we grieve 'cause the future we planned will never happen.

Kassie didn't say anything. She sat there quietly thinking. She had made all of these plans in her head about how life would be when her little sister was born. Instead of having fun with a dear, little, fat, giggling baby, she had ended up with a little sister who looked like an orange, wrinkly, monkey. Instead of being able to cuddle and play with her, she had only been able to stare at her through the glass box. Instead of her smiling and giggling, she had only made a noise when she cried and even then it was a weird high-pitched non-human sort of wail. Nothing had happened the way she had imagined it and now her little sister was dead.

'This is all my fault,' said Kassie.

'Rubbish!' said Gran.

Kassie turned to face Gran, her heart thumping in her chest.

'NO, Gran, you don't understand . . . it IS my fault. I called her a monkey baby. I hated her. She took everyone I love away from me. I didn't wish she was dead, but I may as well have . . . and now she is. Now I can't get her back. Now I'll never play with her, never hug her, never do all the things . . .' Kassie put her head in her hands and cried. She cried so hard she thought her throat would split.

WHAT CAN HELP
- Write a letter to the person who died.
- Look at their photo.
- Tell stories about them to others.
- Make a scrapbook of memories.

Gran put her hand under Kassie's chin and lifted her face. She looked deep into her eyes.

'Now you listen to me, Kassie. This was nobody's fault. Elise was just too little and too weak to fight off the infection. That's ALL. It had nothing to do with you, nothing at all.'

Kassie nodded and looked down again. Gran could say whatever she liked but Kassie KNEW it was her fault. She had been jealous of her little sister and Dad and Mum both knew it too. They would never forgive her. Nothing would ever be the same again.

Q—WILL THEY EVER FORGIVE ME?

A

You are the only one who can forgive yourself. Often we feel guilty for ages because we wait for someone else to tell us not to worry. If you feel guilty, the first thing to do is to try and change things. Do this the best way you can. If the person you feel guilty about has died, respect their memory, talk about them, learn from the life they lived, remember them. Then you need to forgive yourself. No one else can do this for you.

WHAT CAN HELP

- Write: 'I forgive myself' in big letters on a piece of paper or cardboard, decorate it and stick it on the wall in your room to remind yourself.
- Say 'I forgive myself' out loud.
- Say 'I forgive myself' as often as you need to. Whenever thoughts or feelings of guilt sneak into your mind say it again and mean it, 'I forgive myself.'

Now you can start afresh, being more thoughtful, more caring and thankful to the person who died for teaching you this most valuable lesson.

IF YOU'RE BLAMING YOURSELF — — — — — — — — —

Sometimes we blame ourselves when someone we love dies. We regret things we said or didn't say. We feel guilty for things we did or didn't do. Maybe we said something mean to them, or ignored them. Maybe we had an argument and didn't have a chance to apologise. Maybe we never told them that we loved them.

These feelings of regret can trick us into thinking the death was our fault. We might think we are being punished or that we are in some way responsible for their death. If we have had hurtful thoughts and feelings about the person who died, we can think we somehow caused their death.

Our thoughts do not cause someone to die. They die because they are sick.

We might feel guilty for not having done enough. For not telling them how much we love them or how we appreciate what they do for us. Maybe we feel guilty for not reminding them to be careful, or to exercise, or to eat healthy food. All these thoughts and feelings mean we did love them and that we would give anything to have them back again and change how we treated them.

If you feel like this there are a number of things you can do. You could write a letter telling the person how you feel and put it into their coffin. Or you could put the letter in a safe place and every time you're feeling bad, take it out and read it out loud. You could paint a picture of how you wish you'd spent their last days with them. You could make something for them and bury it in the garden. You could sit quietly in a place where you feel safe and just talk to them, tell them how you feel. The important thing is to do SOMETHING. Don't just try and forget these feelings because they'll keep coming back. It's never too late to change how you treat someone, even if they've died.

> Dear Elise,
> It's your big sister writing to you. I just want you to know I love you and I miss you. I'm so sorry for calling you a monkey baby but I never got to know you. All I saw was your little wrinkly body in that glass box. I wanted to play with you, to laugh, to teach you to talk and sing 'Alexander Beetle'. I wanted to show you off to my friends, and when you got bigger share secrets with you. I wanted to tell you about boys and school and bands. I thought we'd have a long life together, and when I got married you could babysit my kids and I'd check out your boyfriends and make sure they looked after you.
>
> Now I'm just sad that we won't have that. I'll never have a little sister and Mum and Dad will never be the same. I wish you had stayed here and if it's my fault that you didn't, please forgive me. I'm so sorry.
> Love, Kassie

CHAPTER 7

HELP! —

Dean knew what today was. It was the day he should have been going on school camp. Instead he was stuck at home minding his little brother because Mum was at work. Everything had changed one day when Dad went off fishing with his mates and never came back. The cops found the boat, but they never found Dad's body. He was probably shark food by now, but Dean would never know. Now he had no life; all he did was jobs around the house, but he couldn't talk about it with Mum because she just got angry and then started bawling. It drove him nuts! How could Dad have done this to him?

Dean and his dad were great mates. They didn't do the sort of stuff that other guys did with their dads, like playing footy or cricket, 'cause Dean's dad wasn't the sporty type, which suited Dean fine—he wasn't the sporty type either. Dean's dad was a journalist, which meant he wrote stories. He always said he 'wrote stories about normal people in extraordinary circumstances'. Dean loved listening to Dad's stories. He knew more about the world than anyone else Dean knew. He could ask Dad anything and mostly he'd know the answer, but if he didn't he could find out quicker than Dean could by Googling.

Dad was a pretty happy sort of bloke, but sometimes a darkness would come over him and he would lock himself in his study for days at a time. Dad called this the 'black dog' and he told Dean, 'When the black dog barks, mate, I just have to lock myself away and write it out.'

Dean never understood this when he was little, so he would knock on the door of the study and call out to Dad.

'Come on, Dad, let's do something.'

But Dad didn't answer. When Dean put his ear up to the door all he could hear was the faint sound of music. Strange, haunting music.

Mum took Dean aside one day and explained to him that when Dad was busy with the black dog it was important to leave him alone until he was ready to come back out. After this, Dad painted a picture of a menacing black dog that looked like a wolf and framed it. He told Dean that when he hung this on the study door it meant he wasn't to be disturbed. And this was the signal they'd used ever since.

WHAT CAN HELP

Everyone deals with their problems in different ways. For some people it is important to have time alone and this can be hard for the people around them. There are a number of ways you can deal with this:

1. Understand that it is not because of you, but that this is how the person thinks through their problems.
2. Talk about it with the person when they have had their time alone.
3. Think about how you deal with your problems and how this might impact on the people around you.

The black dog wasn't too demanding—he only called Dad every so often—and when Dad emerged, though he always looked tired and pale he would bring with him hundreds of new stories and ideas for the books he said he'd write one day. Some of these were the stories he shared with Dean.

Dean was his critic, Dad said. So they would spend hours together reading through the stories. Dean would make suggestions and ask questions and Dad would take his red pencil and cross out words and add in new ones.

'This is a team effort, mate,' he'd say. But there were some stories that remained sealed in a red folder that he wouldn't share, and Dean knew better than to ask why.

'The black dog keeps some of the stories to himself,' Dad would say if he saw Dean looking at the red folder.

Dean loved to write, and as he got older, when Dad retired into the study behind the black dog sign, Dean would go into his room, log on to his computer and write too. Dean's stories were different to Dad's. Dean wrote about imaginary countries, creatures and dark, menacing enemies led by the king of the evil forces, Black Dog. These were the stories *he* didn't share. These were the stories that represented the battle within himself as he grew older: the war between his good and bad self. Somehow writing it all down helped him to think things through. When his mates at school were caught shoplifting, he wrote about this in his imaginary world. When he took $50 from his mum's purse without telling her, he wrote about that. The stories helped him to work out how to deal with the pressures of school, booze, sex, drugs; all the things that a fifteen-year-old guy has to deal with on a daily basis.

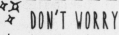

DON'T WORRY
We all need our own time and space to make sense of the world. Writing stories can be a good way of thinking things through.

The kids at school all thought Dean was a bit of a nerd, but that was OK. He had a couple of friends who were collectively referred to by the other kids as the arty-farty crew: the painters, sculptors, drama and music guys who wanted to have careers in the art and theatre world. They were pretty tolerant of diversity and Dean fitted in well with them. Alex in particular spent a lot of time with Dean. Everyone thought they were an item, but they were really just friends. Alex enjoyed writing, too—she wrote poetry.

REMEMBER
We need to remember that we're all different. The world wouldn't work at all (and would be very boring) if everyone was, say, a sportsperson or a musician. There'd be no one to grow food, build houses, care for the sick or govern countries!

When Dad was busy with the black dog Dean began to spend time with Alex, talking about stories, stanzas, haikus and proofreading each other's work. But there were some stories Dean couldn't share, not even with Alex. Stories he knew were too dark to share with anyone. Stories that opened a window into his soul. He wondered if one day, like his dad, these would be his black dog stories.

Dean's little brother, Joe, was a pain. He'd just started high school and hung out with the jocks so he thought he was sick. Whenever Dean was talking about stories with Dad, Joe would start stirring.

DON'T WORRY
When other people don't understand us they can be cruel. This doesn't mean they don't love us, just that they don't understand us.

'What sort of girls are you two with your little stories?' he'd snicker.

Dad just laughed, but it really made Dean angry. Joe needed a good reality check. What was worse, Mum pandered to him like he was an angel. If only she knew what he did behind her back. Dean avoided him as much as he could and spent his time doing his own thing.

One day Dean came running in the door after school and bounded up the stairs to Dad's study. The door was open, so he went straight in. Dad was sitting on his chair with his feet up on the desk.

'What's up, mate?' he asked without looking up from the manuscript in his hand.

'Dad, there's a school camp coming up . . .'

'Thought you weren't into that sort of stuff?' said Dad, finally looking up at Dean over the top of his glasses.

'No, Dad,' he laughed, 'it's an arts camp. There are painters, sculptors and writers coming. Dad, famous writers!' Dean was so excited he could hardly get his words out.

'That's great, mate,' Dad said, as he put down his manuscript and turned towards Dean. 'Tell me all about it.'

Dean thought about that day often. He'd spent ages with Dad talking about what he needed to get for the camp, the questions he should ask the writers. Dad helped him make a long list. In fact, Dad said he was sorry he wasn't going himself. But Dean never got to go to the camp. Only days after spending this wonderful afternoon together, Dad was gone.

WHAT CAN HELP
Our memories link us to the person who died. By thinking about what we did together we keep those memories alive.

It was all so unexpected. Dean thought he was joking when Dad told him he was going fishing with some mates.

'Fishing, Dad?' he asked.

'Yep, mate, fishing. Do you believe it? I don't even know how to bait a hook!'

'So why are you going?' Dean asked, still not believing what he was hearing.

'Some guys from work asked me to go, so I thought I should. I never go to those work things. Your school camp encouraged me to go,' he said.

'What do ya mean?'

'Well, I thought if you were brave enough to go to the school camp, I should be brave enough to go fishing!'

Dean remembered how uncomfortable Dad looked the morning he headed off on the fishing trip. He was carrying a rod and a small esky filled with sandwiches he'd made. He was wearing an old pair of jeans and his gardening jumper. He looked so uncomfortable.

'Have fun, Dad!' Dean said as he headed out the door.

Mum laughed and said, 'Make sure you bring home plenty of fish for dinner.'

Nothing out of the ordinary happened that day, until the evening news came on the television. Joe was sitting playing on his laptop when Dean heard him call out to Mum.

'Hey, Mum, where'd the old man go fishing?'

'Down the Peninsula, Joe,' Mum called back from the kitchen.

The hair on the back of Dean's neck stood up on end and he suddenly felt like he would throw up. Something was wrong. He couldn't put his finger on it, but he felt like there was a black shadow sitting around him.

The police arrived about an hour later. They never found Dad's body. The search and rescue cops looked for a week. Divers, helicopters and everything. Dad was the only one who wasn't rescued; the other three guys were found clinging to the upturned hull of the boat but, search as they did, they didn't find Dad.

DON'T WORRY
We all grieve differently. But sometimes it can be hard to understand why someone else behaves the way they do.

Mum locked herself in her room for days. When she finally came out she just cried or lost her temper. Joe was his usual abrasive self and even said he was sure that Dad had topped himself.

Mum eventually went back to work. 'Someone has to pay the bloody bills,' she said. And Dean had to do all the housework and try to keep Joe under control. Dean's life had changed and yet he still couldn't really believe Dad was dead. The funeral was bizarre 'cause there was no coffin. Joe kept saying that Dad had gone to catch fish and because he was so useless the fish had caught him. Dean wanted to punch him, but he didn't.

DON'T WORRY
When a parent dies we often end up with a whole lot of extra responsibilities that can make it hard to find the time to do the things that make us feel good. We need to try and make time for those things.

The day Dean was supposed to go on the school camp he felt really angry. He sat in his room with the list of questions he'd written with Dad. He had no time to spend writing any more. By the time he'd done his homework, the housework, cooked dinner and tried to control Joe, there was no spare time at all. He didn't even get to hang out with Alex. He screwed up the list of questions and threw them in the corner.

Dean sat in his room thinking about his dad. He was angry with him. WHY did he have to go fishing? It was so unlike him. Dean started to wonder. What if Joe was right? He went up to Dad's study and opened the door. The room was exactly as Dad had left it. He grabbed the black dog painting off the shelf and walked over to the door and hung it on the nail. He shut the door and turned the key in the lock.

He sat down in his dad's chair and, reaching over to the filing cabinet, picked up the red folder that was sitting on top of a big pile of papers. He leaned back in his dad's chair, put his feet on the desk, opened the folder and began to read.

YOU'RE NOT ALONE

For Dean,

The contents of this folder are my innermost and personal thoughts, feelings, stories and ideas. They have evolved during my periods of enforced seclusion over many years. The pain, the anguish and the sadness are all here, but form only a small part of this collection. The bulk of this work is about the kindness, generosity, compassion and love I have experienced throughout my life.

I trust you with this, my life story, Dean, because I know you understand. You are a fine writer, I am so proud of you. You can change the world and I'll always be by your side.

All my love,

Dad

This very first page told Dean a huge amount about his dad, but the thing that comforted him the most was the date at the bottom of the dedication page: 'January 2005', five years ago.

Q–WHERE CAN I GO TO GET HELP?

A

There are lots of places you can go for help if you are finding things hard. The best place to start is to talk to someone you trust. This could be an adult in your family, even if they are struggling themselves. Sometimes when we are grieving we are so wound up in our own sorrow we forget that others are having a hard time too. So start by talking to a parent or close family member. You could also talk to someone at school you feel comfortable with, a teacher, school counsellor or school chaplain.

There are also people in your community who will help you. Your local doctor is a good person to talk to 'cause they understand, and if you need some time with someone who only works with grieving people your doctor can point you in the right direction.

The important thing to remember is that you don't have to do this on your own, but you can't wait for someone to notice that you're struggling. Speak up and ask for help.

WHEN THERE ISN'T A BODY — — — — — — — — — —

When the person's body is never found it adds an extra dimension of uncertainty to our grief because there's no proof that the person has died. We often feel like the death is a mistake. It can't have happened. We can't see the body. There's no one to put into a coffin, no one to bury and no place to go to visit them.

WHAT CAN HELP
It can help to make a special place where you can spend time with the person who died. Somewhere in the garden, a special room in the house or maybe a place at the beach or in the park where you may have shared happy times with them.

We imagine that one day the person will just walk in the door like nothing has happened. As the weeks and months go by the reality of the death begins to sink in, but still at the back of our mind is the hope that one day . . .

When someone we love dies unexpectedly and in unusual circumstances we can start to wonder about whether it really was an accident. If the person we love has lived with mental illness or depression we might be tempted to think their death was something they planned. This then starts us asking questions, question after question. But often there are no answers.

If we become totally wound up in trying to find reasons, it makes our grieving more difficult. We can start to blame

REMEMBER
There are many organisations that can provide information about mental illness and depression. BeyondBlue is a good place to start. Go to: <www.beyondblue.org.au>

ourselves, thinking, *I should have noticed something was wrong* or *Why did I leave them alone*? But the truth is, nothing we did or didn't do will change the fact that the person has died. The important thing for us to do is to allow ourselves to grieve, to feel the strong feelings that our grieving brings to the surface even if that means being angry for a while.

WHAT CAN HELP
Writing down our thoughts and feelings can help us understand them.

CHAPTER 8

WHEN WILL THIS BE OVER? – – – – – – – – – –

Jake had a small wooden box wrapped up in a blanket under his bed. It had been there for three years and he got it out every so often. He made sure the house was quiet and that he wouldn't be disturbed. He closed the door to his room, reached under his bed and pulled out the box. He unwrapped it carefully, folding the blanket gently to one side. He put the box on his lap, slowly opened it and looked at what was inside.

He picked up each thing, one at a time. A silver medal, a pair of cufflinks, some copper coins, a yellow billiard ball, a handful of nails and screws, a gold fountain pen and at the very bottom of the box was the greatest treasure of all: an old white hanky with the initials 'HJ' embroidered in blue thread.

He took out the neatly ironed and folded hanky and, putting it to his nose, closed his eyes and took a big

? –
DID YOU KNOW?
Every person has a particular smell that we recognise. A smell that's a mixture of them and hair oil, perfume, powder, soap, any number of things. This smell can live on in things that belonged to them, especially clothes and personal items. **?**

sniff. *Yep*, he thought, the smell was still there, that 'Gag' smell that was a combination of washing powder, starch, aftershave and that special something he found nowhere else—the smell of his grandad.

Gag had always called Jake his little mate. Jake couldn't remember a time when his grandad wasn't around, but now he was gone. Dead. Never to return. That's why the box that lived under Jake's bed was so important. This box created a bridge that Jake could cross whenever he had time to himself. And this bridge transported him to another time and place when things were different. When he lived with Gag, and life was simple. When no matter how naughty he was, Gag always forgave him. 'Now you're a good kid,' he'd say as he tucked Jake into bed.

WHAT CAN HELP

Remembering the times when you had disagreements as well as the times of forgiveness remind us that none of us are perfect, but that we are still loved no matter what.

Gag never had to get really mad at Jake 'cause as soon as he realised Gag was cross, Jake would do whatever he could to fix things. He hated letting Gag down, but sometimes he just got carried away. He'd jump around on the couch, or jump up and down on his bed, or refuse to eat his vegetables, then Gag would yell: 'JAKE, cut it out.' But sometimes he'd just push it that one step too far and end up in the bedroom for time out. Gag would come in and sit on the bed, they would talk quietly together and everything would be all right again.

Jake couldn't remember a time when Gag wasn't there. His earliest memories are of sitting on Gag's knee listening to him tell stories. Gag always told stories. He saved the best ones for after dinner, when he'd had a few beers and was in fine form, as Grandma would say. Then sometimes, especially when there were visitors, Gag would get out his accordion and sing funny old songs. Jake could remember dancing around in the kitchen while Gag sang, his face getting redder and redder as his voice filled up the room. Gag loved to sing, especially when he had an audience, and even though he was old and Jake was little, he knew Gag actually had a fine voice.

It wasn't till Jake got older that he started to wonder about things. He wondered why he and his mum lived with Gag and Grandma. None of the other cousins lived there. Sure they came to visit, but they always went back to their own places. Jake and Mum had their own rooms at Gag and Grandma's. He knew this was their home, yet the older he got the more this seemed a bit strange. One day Jake asked Gag about it, but he said, 'You've always lived here with us, mate, and I'm glad.' So Jake just left it at that.

WHAT HELPED ME

'I remember that daggy dressing gown my dad used to wear. I kept it in the bottom of my wardrobe. No one knew. But it was important to me. It felt like him. It smelled like him.'
Daniel, 13

Gag had always been old. As far back as Jake could remember he'd had white hair. He wore funny old-man pyjamas and a scratchy woollen dressing gown in the mornings when he came out to the kitchen for breakfast. He'd squeeze four oranges into a glass for Jake, then squeeze another four for himself and they'd sit down at the big wooden table together. Sometimes Gag would cook a boiled egg and put Jake on his knee and share the soldiers of toast with him. When Jake was really little, Gag cut up his toast and Vegemite into little squares and fed them to him one at a time. He always pretended to take the last little square and just when he was about to pop it into his mouth, Jake would yell, 'No, Gaggy, that one's mine.'

Gag smiled his funny sideways smile and said, 'Of course it is,' and then dropped it into Jake's mouth like he was feeding a baby bird.

Jake took another sniff of the 'HJ' hanky and remembered the day he realised that Gag was REALLY old. It had happened after Jake started school—on the day of the school sports. Mum, Grandma and Gag had gone to the oval to watch him run. He'd been practising for months, running round and round the backyard. In fact, every time he had too much energy Mum would say, 'Go and do ten laps of the yard, Jake, and run off some of that energy.'

So out to the backyard he'd go and run round until he was exhausted. Now he thought about it, he guessed Mum was just trying to wear him out so he wouldn't jump around in the house so much. Anyway, one afternoon Gag came out to watch him run around the backyard and as he walked along the path, he tripped and fell. Jake ran over to him. 'Gag, you OK?'

WHEN WILL THIS BE OVER?

'Jeepers, I've hurt me foot,' he said. Jake leaned over to try and help him up, but Gag just said, 'Go get Grandma will ya, mate?' and stayed where he was lying on the ground.

When the ambulance came to take Gag to hospital Jake thought he'd never see him again, but he came home after a few days and from then on he had to walk with a stick. On the day of the sports, Jake was getting ready to run his race. He looked over to where Mum, Grandma and Gag were sitting in the shade of a big, old gum tree and that's when he noticed it. Gag was sitting in a fold-up chair leaning on his stick. His head was resting on his arm and Jake all of a sudden noticed how VERY old he looked. Jake waved to Gag. He smiled back, but it was a sort of feeble smile that almost looked like it hurt. But Jake knew it couldn't possibly hurt to smile. Still, Gag's face looked weird and he couldn't quite work it out.

DON'T WORRY
Sometimes we don't notice the people close to us growing older until we look at them in a different way, in a different environment.

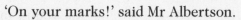

'On your marks!' said Mr Albertson.

Jake stepped up to the white line with six other kids from his grade. He forgot about Gag's weird smile and got ready to run.

That all seemed like so long ago. Jake was fourteen now and Gag had been dead since he was ten. He lived in a new house now. Mum had married a nice guy called

Graham and the three of them lived together just down the road from Grandma's house. Grandma had moved too 'cause she said her old house was just too big for one little old lady.

Jake put the HJ hanky carefully back into the box. He lifted out the medal. He held it in his hand and looked at the gold engraving, Dux 1932. He remembered the day Gag gave it to him. He'd just come home from yet another stay in hospital. Jake had run in the door from school,

'Where's Gag?' he asked Grandma as he ran down the hall to the kitchen.

'Shhhh, love. He's in bed. He's really tired. It's been a long trip from the city,' Grandma said.

DON'T WORRY

Adults sometimes try to warn us that someone we love is sick. They do this to prepare us for the possibility that they might die. It doesn't matter if we know that the dying is coming; when the person dies, no matter how prepared we are, it's still a shock.

'Come and sit down a minute, Jakey,' she said, patting her lap. So Jake walked over to the big chair where Grandma was sitting and sat on her knee. She put her arms around him and squeezed him tightly.

'Gag's not too good, love,' she told him.

'What do you mean? They've sent him home, so he must be better,' Jake said.

'I think he's just as good as he's going to get,' Grandma said softly. 'He's very old, you know.'

'He's always been old,' said Jake. Grandma just smiled and cuddled him again.

When Jake finally went to the bedroom, he popped his head around the door quietly. The room was dark and he could hear Gag breathing noisily.

'That you, mate?' he whispered in a croaky voice.

'Yep, Gag, it's me.'

'Come on in then,' he said.

Jake crept quietly into the room and stood by the bed. Gag sure looked terrible. His face was almost as white as his hair, and his lips were all cracked. He patted the bed next to him and Jake sat down.

That was the afternoon that Gag had given him the medal. He told Jake he'd won it for being the top of the school when he was a kid. He also said that he'd mind it for him for now, but that one day it would belong to Jake and he wanted him to keep it safe. Like a treasure.

DID YOU KNOW?
When someone shares something special with us, whether it's a story, song or a thing that has particular significance to them, they are telling us how much they love us.

Gag had given Jake lots of treasures over the years, things that other people might think were junk but that were special to Jake 'cause they each meant something. He reached into the box and pulled out three Japanese coins. He held them in his hand and remembered the day Gag gave them to him. He'd told Jake about flying to Japan when there was a war happening in Vietnam. Gag said he'd looked out the window of the plane in the dark when everyone else was asleep and saw bombs going off miles below, making beautiful lights like fireworks. He told Jake how sad it made him feel, that while he was up there in the night sky safe and sound, there were people down below being killed. Mothers, fathers, kids, babies, soldiers, farmers, shopkeepers, all dead.

'Just normal people like us, Jake. All being blown up. Their houses destroyed. Their lives ruined. War is a terrible thing, mate, never forget that.' And Jake never had forgotten. Every time he picked up those coins, he remembered. He gently put the coins back into the box.

Next Jake pulled out a yellow billiard ball, rolled it around in his hand and smiled. 'The bathplug,' he whispered. Jake loved Gag very much, but knew he was a bit of a bad sport. Whenever he played billiards or pool, he played to win and got very grumpy if he didn't. Gag blamed 'the bathplug' every time he lost.

'It's that bloody bathplug,' Gag said. 'It's got it in for me!'

Jake never understood why Gag called it 'the bathplug' until he was older and realised that Gag was too polite to say 'bastard', so he called the yellow ball 'the bathplug' instead. Jake laughed as he put 'the bathplug' back into the box.

> **REMEMBER**
> Things don't have to be worth lots of money to be treasures. Treasures are treasures because they mean something special to us.

Jake took out three bent screws and felt their sharp points. Gag was good at lots of things, but building wasn't one of them. The day he bent the screws, Jake had spent ages sitting on an old, wobbly chair in the shed while Gag was trying to fix the shelves where he stacked all his tools. Jake never quite understood why Gag had so many tools 'cause every time he tried to fix something it never looked right. The shed was full of cupboards, tables, chairs and a bookcase that Gag had tried to fix. They were all crooked and bent, but Gag wouldn't throw them away. He said they were all 'perfectly good, Grandma is just too fussy!'

Jake handed screws to Gag, one at a time. Every time Gag bent one, he dropped it on the ground and put out his hand for another one. The ground beneath Jake's wobbly chair was littered with bent screws.

'Bloody screws,' said Gag. 'They don't make things like they used to, mate.'

Finally, Gag looked at his watch. 'Must be lunchtime,' he said. 'We'll finish this later.'

'Can I have some of these screws, Gag?' Jake asked.

'Sure, mate, take as many as you like, but don't let Grandma find them,' he said with a wink. Gag rubbed Jake's hair and waited for him as he picked the three most bent screws and put them into his pocket.

YOU'RE NOT ALONE

After someone we love dies, we may find ourselves saying things they would have said or using funny words or phrases they used to use. When we hear ourselves say these things, it reminds us of them.

'Don't toss me hair,' Jake said, laughing. This was one of Gag's famous sayings. He hated it when anyone touched his perfectly combed white hair.

'Ha!' said Gag.

Jake dropped the screws back into the wooden box. There were only three things left that he hadn't held in his hands. He picked up the pair of beautiful blue and gold cufflinks. He'd worn these cufflinks to Gag's funeral. Jake remembered the day Gag died.

DON'T WORRY

When we know someone is dying and it takes ages, we can sometimes wish it was over. For them and for us. When the person does die, we may feel bad 'cause we wanted it to hurry up.

We don't need to feel bad. We wanted it to hurry so the person we love wouldn't suffer.

Gag had been in hospital for weeks. He'd been very sick and every time Jake visited, Gag would fall asleep while he was in the middle of talking. Sometimes what he said made absolutely no sense. Mum explained to Jake that Gag was dying, but it seemed to be taking ages. No one could say when it would happen, so Grandma told Mum to take Jake on the holiday they had been planning and that she would ring if anything changed. Jake and Mum headed off in the car so early in the morning it was still dark. When they stopped at a little country town for lunch, Mum's mobile rang.

It took five hours for Mum and Jake to get back to the hospital. Grandma and all the family were sitting around Gag's bed. Jake remembered cuddling Gag and telling him he loved him. Gag didn't open his eyes. His mouth was open and his pale hands were all floppy. Within minutes he just stopped breathing.

Jake closed his eyes. He could still see a picture in his mind of what Gag looked like lying dead in that hospital bed. He felt like he was back in that room, and started to feel sad.

Suddenly there was a knock on the door. 'You in there, Jake?'

Jake jumped as Mum walked in.

'What are you doing there, love?' Mum asked as she sat down on the floor next to him.

'Just thinking about Gag,' he said.

'You feeling sad?' asked Mum.

'Nope, just wanted to remember his face. Sometimes I try and I just can't get the picture in my head. Looking at this stuff helps,' Jake said as he put the cufflinks back into the box.

WHAT CAN HELP

Anything that can help you keep the picture of the person's face in your mind . . . is a treasure.

Mum watched Jake carefully rearrange the pieces of Gag's life he had collected.

'See that gold pen?' she asked. 'I remember the day Gag got that pen. He'd just retired,' Mum said.

Jake picked up the long, thin gold pen and handed it to Mum. She smiled as she turned the pen around in her hand. Then she laughed.

'What's so funny?' Jake asked.

'He wasn't very impressed,' Mum said.

'Why?' asked Jake.

'It's a long story,' said Mum.

'Tell me,' Jake responded as he leaned back against the side of his bed and waited for Mum to begin.

Q – WILL OTHER PEOPLE THINK I DON'T CARE IF I START TO FEEL HAPPY AGAIN?

A

Everyone takes their own time to start feeling happy. At some stage you will start to enjoy the normal things in life again, like hanging out with friends or playing sport, the stuff you used to do before. That doesn't mean you don't miss the person who has died. It just means that YOU are still living and because you are still living you'll experience all the feelings that go with living: good and bad, happy and sad.

Some people take longer than others to let themselves feel happy again and that's OK. Everyone does it in their own time.

FEELING HAPPY AGAIN — — — — — — — — — — — — —

Our life changes forever when someone we love dies. There's a big piece that will never be the way it was because someone is missing.

The grief we feel will ease over time and we will function again, but differently. The tears won't be so frequent, we'll go back to school, to our jobs and to our life, but there will always be a hole, a space that used to be filled by the person who died. We will be able to laugh, have fun and be happy again and we will be able to remember the person or relationship happily even though we still miss them.

There will be times when we still feel sad, but the sadness changes too. In the beginning it may feel like our heart has been ripped apart, a pain that's so awful nothing can make it go away. But after a while the sad moments get jumbled up with the happy memories and we'll find ourselves laughing and crying all at once.

The tears we'll cry now feel different. They are almost comforting. These tears tell us that we're still connected to the person we love who died. Even though we can't touch them we can see them in our mind, hear their voice in our head and know that they will always be part of us. That's why the treasures we keep that belonged to the person are so important. These things help us to keep our memories alive.

CHAPTER 9

REMEMBERING — — — — — — — — — — — — — —

It was 5 January. For the past three years every 5 January had been the same, but in some ways a little different each year. The first year it was filled with tears, sadness and misery, but as the years went by there was also laughter, smiles and a warm fuzzy feeling. Sally used to dread 5 January but gradually she found herself looking forward to it. While all her friends were at the beach or hanging out at the pool, she would visit the cemetery and then have a family dinner at home surrounded by photos and listening to the music her dad, Chester, loved to sing along to. After dinner she'd put on a thick pair of black rimmed glasses and read the newspaper.

5 January, Chester-day.

When her dad died, it was like the world changed forever. Everything she had depended on. Every hope she had for the future. Everything that made her life HER life was gone. Sally loved her dad and she missed him. She missed throwing hoops with him in the backyard. She missed his lame jokes. She missed the smell of his favourite aftershave. And she missed the funny way he rubbed his eyebrow with his finger when he read the newspaper. The house just wasn't the same without him.

Sally was the only girl in her family and she was the youngest. She had three older brothers but only Gus was still living at home. Dave and Thomas were both married. The boys always told Sally she was a mistake because there was such a big gap in their ages, but Dad told Sally that he and Mum had tried one last time to get a girl. Sally's mum died when she was just a baby so she'd spent her whole life being 'the lady of the house', as Dad liked to call her.

For as long as Sally could remember Beth lived in the house next door. She lived in a beautiful little green and white cottage surrounded by trees and flowers in the front and filled with vegetable beds in the back. When Sally was little, Beth minded her after school and in the holidays while Dad was at work. Sally called her Aunty Beth even though she was no relation, 'cause Dad said it was impolite for kids to call old ladies by their first name. Since Sally had grown older, she just called her Beth and no one seemed to mind.

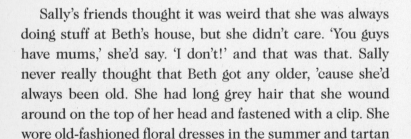

DON'T WORRY
Sometimes our friends don't understand when we choose to spend time with other people, especially if they are older.

Sally's friends thought it was weird that she was always doing stuff at Beth's house, but she didn't care. 'You guys have mums,' she'd say. 'I don't!' and that was that. Sally never really thought that Beth got any older, 'cause she'd always been old. She had long grey hair that she wound around on the top of her head and fastened with a clip. She wore old-fashioned floral dresses in the summer and tartan skirts and cardies in the winter. And in the garden, she wore an apron over her clothes and gumboots on her feet.

Sally always helped Beth with the garden. When she was little Beth taught her how to plant seedlings and gently water them with a watering can. Later, she taught Sally how to prune the fruit trees and take cuttings from the roses. Sally loved hanging out in the garden, getting her hands dirty and learning about how things grow.

Beth taught her about plants that were used for medicine and about herbs that were used to make therapeutic oils. Lavender, thyme, sage and rosemary. 'Rosemary is for remembering, Sal, don't forget that,' she'd say, giggling.

One day when she told Sally about rosemary for the millionth time, she laughed so hard that she lost her balance and fell into the compost heap. Sally laughed till she had tears in her eyes.

Beth was a great cook, too. She taught Sally how to bake cakes and puddings. They must have tasted great 'cause when she brought them home the boys ate them without leaving a crumb. In the late summer they'd spend hours making tomato sauce, lemon cordial and jam, mostly plum and raspberry. Raspberry was Dad's favourite.

Sally loved Beth's house. Not just because of the garden, but inside the house was crammed full of stuff— girlie stuff. Timber furniture, leather chairs, embroidered rugs, painted china cups and little statues filled every corner. The kitchen walls were covered with shelves that were filled with jars of jam, sauce and dried fruit, and herbs were always hanging in the pantry cupboard.

Beth didn't have a TV, but she had more books than Sally had ever seen in the one place except maybe the school library. The house was always cool in summer and warm in winter. It was a sort of haven for a girl like Sally, who didn't have a mum.

Sally never could work out why the time seemed to fly so fast when she was next door with Beth. She'd go through the garden gate thinking she'd only stay for a little while, but before she knew it the sun had dropped in the sky and it was time to go home for dinner. The only day of the year she didn't go through the gate was on 19 March, Beth-day. This was the day Beth always spent alone.

Every year for as long as Sally had known her, she had never seen her on Beth-day. Sally asked Beth about it once and she just said, 'Beth-day is the one day a year I need to spend on my own, Sally. It's my day.' So Sally never asked about it again, but she never looked forward to Beth-day 'cause as it got closer, Beth seemed to get further away.

One summer evening Sally and Beth were standing at the gate, talking.

'What do you two girls get up to in there all day?' Dad asked as he wandered up the yard towards them.

'Never you mind, Chester!' said Beth.

'Secret women's business, eh?' chuckled Dad.

'Yeah,' said Sally.

It was Beth who talked to Sally about growing up. She told her about puberty and sex. At first Sally thought Beth was making it up, but she soon realised she wasn't. Sally felt comfortable with Beth. She could ask her about anything and she did. One early summer evening they were kneeling together in the yard pulling up carrots and Beth said, 'Sal, you really need to start spending more time with your friends.'

Sally leaned back on her heels, 'What do ya mean, Beth? You sick of me?'

Beth leaned back on her heels, too. 'Of course not! I just worry a bit about you spending so much time hanging round with an old lady, that's all. You're not a kid any more, Sal.'

Beth was right about both things. Sally was thirteen. She'd got her period ages ago and had been wearing a bra since she was twelve. She was grown up. Maybe she should spend more time with her friends.

'I've got all the summer holidays coming up, I'll do it then,' Sally said.

The summer holidays didn't turn out how Sally had imagined. They'd had a wonderful Christmas, the whole family together. Sally cooked the roast dinner and Beth came over in the evening to see how she was going with the pudding. The boys all said Sally was a wonderful cook and sat around holding their stomachs, groaning.

'Oh, I'm gonna explode.'

'Ooh, Christmas disease.'

'Well, that's what happens when you eat too much!' Sally teased them.

Dad died on 5 January. He'd gone up the street to get the paper and just dropped dead outside the newsagent. The doctor said he was dead before he hit the ground, but that didn't make Sally feel any better.

That first year after Dad died went past in a whirl. There was the invasion of relatives Sally had never met, coming to pay their respects. There were arguments with Dave and Thomas, who both wanted to sell the house and have Sally live with them. Luckily Dad had written a will that said Sally and Gus were to stay in the house for as long as they wanted to. So that's what happened. Beth-day came and went and Sally didn't even notice. Life went on for everyone else, but not for Sally.

When someone we love dies, things that may have seemed important before can just slip past unnoticed. Nothing is the same as it was.

The first Christmas without Dad was awful. Sally and Gus set up the tree, but the lights wouldn't work properly. Sally set the table for dinner but Dad's place was empty. She cooked a roast dinner and pudding but no one was hungry. Dave and Thomas left early 'cause they said they were tired. Gus sat staring at Christmas carols on the TV. Sally went into her room, sat on the bed and stared out the window into Beth's backyard.

REMEMBER
Special days like Christmas, birthdays and anniversaries can be very hard times for people after the death of someone close. No matter what they do, there is something missing . . . there's a big hole where the person they love should be, an empty place at the table that no one else can fill.

The next day Sally went through the gate in the fence to the house next door. Beth was in the kitchen wrapping up some shortbread into little parcels.

'I was hoping you'd come over today, Sal,' she said.

'Why didn't you come to our place last night, Beth?' she blurted out. 'I waited and you didn't come. You always come on Christmas night.'

Beth wiped her hands on a tea towel. 'Sit down, Sal, we need to talk.'

Sally sat down on her favourite wooden chair and Beth poured two glasses of cordial from the jug sitting on the bench. She put them on the table and sat down too. She let out a big sigh and leaned her elbows on the tabletop.

'When I was seven my mother died,' she said.

'Oh, that's awful,' Sally replied.

'It was awful, Sal, but what was worse, I didn't even know she was sick. I went home from school one day for lunch and there was a car I didn't know parked in front of our house. I ran inside all excited.'

'Who was it?' asked Sally.

'My dad's brother. I'd never met him before. He lived far away in the country.' Beth sighed again. 'My dad told me I was so lucky 'cause I was going on a holiday. My bag was packed and Uncle Bob was hurrying me to get ready to leave 'cause it was a long drive, and he wanted to get home before dark.'

'Were you scared?' Sally asked.

'A little, but Dad kept saying Uncle Bob had lots of kids and I'd have a great time.'

'Anyway, I wanted to kiss Mum goodbye, but Dad said she was having a rest. He patted me on the head and told me to have fun and Uncle Bob bundled me into the car and off we went.' Beth looked into her lap and didn't say anything.

'Then what happened?' asked Sally.

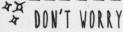

DON'T WORRY

Sometimes when people try to protect us from something painful by sending us away or excluding us, it makes things much, much worse.

'I never saw my mum again. I was gone for three months and when Uncle Bob finally took me home, Mum was gone, her clothes were gone, her photos were gone. Every little piece of her that had been in that house was gone.' Beth took a deep breath.

'I ran around and around the house calling to her till Dad grabbed me by the shoulders and shook me. He shook me hard and said, "She's DEAD, Elizabeth. She's never coming back".' Beth slumped back into her chair. 'I was seven years old, Sal. I didn't understand "dead".'

'Oh Beth, that sucks,' said Sally, not knowing what else to say.

 It doesn't matter how old we are, painful memories are always painful.

'Yes, Sal, sometimes life just sucks,' Beth said sadly. She sat quietly and Sally noticed a tear on her cheek. Beth pulled her hanky out of her apron pocket and wiped the tear away, then she turned to Sally and looked deeply into her eyes.

'That's why Beth-day is so important,' she said

'Beth-day? What's it got to do with Beth-day?' asked Sally.

'Beth-day is the one day each year I spend with Mum—19 March every year since I was eight.' Beth seemed to be thinking aloud. 'I guess that's a lot of years.' She added, 'You see, Sal, she was Beth too.'

Beth told Sally how she had been angry with her dad until he was very old and he finally told her why he'd sent her away. He told Beth that all of the relatives said it would be better for her if she didn't watch her mother dying. That she'd get over it quicker. He was sad because he knew sending her away had made it worse, not better.

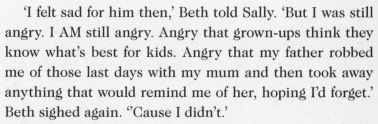

SAD MOMENT
'When everyone else thinks they know what I need without asking me.'
Nathan, 15

'I felt sad for him then,' Beth told Sally. 'But I was still angry. I AM still angry. Angry that grown-ups think they know what's best for kids. Angry that my father robbed me of those last days with my mum and then took away anything that would remind me of her, hoping I'd forget.' Beth sighed again. ''Cause I didn't.'

Beth and Sally sat quietly at the kitchen table. Sally didn't know whether to say anything or not. She was still a bit confused about why Beth had told her all this. So she sat and let her own thoughts occupy her mind. She was thinking about Christmas Day. About Dad's empty place at the table. About how much of a hole it leaves when someone you love dies. About how she never knew her mum, but somehow she still missed her. No mum and now no dad.

'Sal, other people can't make you forget you know. You only forget if *you* let yourself.' Beth stood up and put her hand on Sally's shoulder.

'Guess I should show you how I remember. It might help you.'

Q-WHAT IF I DON'T WANT TO GO TO THE FUNERAL?

A

The main reason we don't want to go to the funeral is because we're scared. We don't know what to expect. We might be scared of the idea of being surrounded by sad people. We might be scared about what happens at a funeral because we've never been to one before. The formality of it might scare us or we could be scared 'cause we don't want to cry in public.

If we remember *why* we're going to the funeral, this can help. Being focused on remembering and celebrating the life of the person we love can make it easier for us. Funerals are also an important way for the community to support grieving families and friends. They allow workmates, colleagues, community leaders and other people to say 'we will miss this person' and 'we are here to support you' just by attending the funeral.

Going to a funeral should always be a personal choice. We should never be *forced* to go to a funeral, just as we should never be *stopped* from going as it is an important part of our grieving process.

FINDING WAYS OF REMEMBERING— — — — — — — —

It is important to have ways of remembering the person who has died. Funerals, memorials, photos, songs and rituals help to keep the memory alive.

The whole idea of a funeral can be really hard to get our head around, partly because they happen so soon after the death of the person we love. We will still be in the grip of terrible sadness and feelings of disbelief, and so the funeral may go by in a blur. Sometimes people think that if they have the funeral quickly, then everyone can start getting over the impact the death has had on their lives. But this isn't true.

The funeral plays a very important role for all the people who attend. Just as a christening or naming ceremony welcomes a new baby to the world surrounded by those who are celebrating the birth, a funeral farewells the person who has died. It's an opportunity to celebrate the life of the person and say goodbye. And to learn things about them—and ourselves—that we may not have known before. It's also an opportunity

WHAT CAN HELP
Things you can do to make the funeral meaningful for you:
- read a favourite poem;
- play a favourite song;
- tell a story;
- put a symbol on the coffin;
- pick a bunch of special flowers.

for us to comfort and support each other. To say in a formal way, 'We loved this person too and we are here to support you.'

Funerals tell the story of the person's life in words, symbols and song. They include the things that were important to the person during their life. Some people choose to have funerals in a church, because this may have been an important part of the person's life. Others choose to have funerals in a hall or in the bush or on the beach or in a park, because these places may better reflect the life of the person who died.

DID YOU KNOW?
There are no rules about when or where the funeral is held. It's up to the family and close friends to make these decisions.

Sometimes people bring symbols of the person's life and lay them on the coffin or on a table nearby. Musical instruments, treasures, tools they may have used in their job, sports jumpers, a typewriter or paintbrushes: symbols that tell the story of the person. Often a big photo of the person is displayed, or a DVD will be played along with their favourite music. There's no right or wrong way of doing this, so long as we have an opportunity to share what we thought was important about the life of the person we loved.

In the years that follow, we may choose to mark the anniversary of the person's death by visiting their grave, by going to a place where they liked to hang out, by planting a tree or by having a special meal at home with family and friends. These types of rituals keep the memory of the person alive by continuing to celebrate their lives and tell their story to others.

CHAPTER 10

WHO AM I REALLY? — — — — — — — — — — — — — — —

Lou felt sick every morning when she woke up. She had been to the doctor a million times and he kept saying it was 'all in her head'.

'How can it be in my head?' she said. 'Sometimes I actually spew!'

Lou knew when it had all started, but she wasn't telling the stupid doctor that she'd seen the old man hit by the train; after all, he was just some homeless guy who hung around in the park. She didn't even know him.

Everything had been fine before that. She'd lived in the same place for as long as she could remember. Just her and Mum in their cute little house covered in ivy. That's how it had always been. Lou loved living in their country town. It was the best of both worlds. She walked to school in summer, listening to the cicadas making their loud ringing noises in the trees that lined the park at the end of the street. In winter she loved curling up next to the fire and watching TV with Mum. She loved her school and had a pile of friends she'd known for years. They spent the summers at the pool and their winters watching the local football and going to the snow, which was only an hour's drive from home.

Lou never understood why people said being a teenager was crap. She was nearly fifteen and so far all it had meant was an occasional pimple and getting used to getting her period every month. Lou knew she was lucky 'cause some of her friends weren't finding it so easy. Her friend Jess had terrible acne and Lou knew that it made her feel really bad, especially when guys from the pub called her 'pizza face'. Lou's other friend Marnie had started sneaking out at night and going to parties down at the caravan park. Lou knew she was drinking a lot and guessed she was doing drugs as well—Marnie hardly came to school any more, and whenever Lou saw her down the street she looked terrible. Lou almost felt guilty that her life was so normal.

REMEMBER

We all deal with life stresses differently. Some of us drift into destructive ways of trying to come to terms with changes in our lives. If you feel that you're not coping, always ask someone you trust for help.

Lou had never met her dad. When she was little she wished he would show up on the doorstep one day and say he wanted them all to be a family. She'd got over that now and even thought that if he did turn up, it might actually wreck things. Lou and Mum were fine on their own. No fights, no aggro, just a normal, happy life. The sort of life everyone should be able to have.

Old Tom just arrived in the park one day with a pile of newspapers, a cardboard box and three green garbage bags full of tins. No one took much notice of him at first, then one day he started yelling out at people as they walked past.

'Tom's an old bastard. That's what ya think, innit?'

He always yelled the same thing, though sometimes he changed the order of the words so it made no sense at all: 'Old Tom's, bastard, innit? That's what ya think.'

He'd yell at anyone who came near the seat he sat on all day and slept on at night. That's why people started calling him 'Old Tom'. Lou didn't know if that was his real name, but then it didn't really matter.

Lou felt sorry for Old Tom, but he scared her too. His hair was long and scraggly, his coat was all dirty and torn and he never wore shoes. But it was the yelling that scared her the most. She knew he was harmless, but she just didn't feel comfortable with aggro and never had. She and Mum never got angry with each other and Lou always felt anxious when people around her got angry, even her friends.

DON'T WORRY

We tend to be frightened of things we don't understand. It can sometimes be hard to understand people whose lives are very different from our own.

'I just don't like conflict,' she'd say to them, which always made them laugh.

Peace, that's all I want, she thought.

Old Tom had been living in the park for a few months. Every so often the council men would come and try to move him off, but the next day he'd be back on his seat again yelling at anyone who'd listen. In the end, they just gave up and left him alone. People in the town had got used to Old Tom and it was like he'd been there forever.

The weather had started to get colder and he'd taken to lighting a fire each night in the rubbish bin at the edge of the park. He'd spend the afternoon staggering around under the trees collecting sticks and rotted branches and hiding them under his seat so that once it got dark he had fuel for his fire.

One cool autumn afternoon Lou was walking home from school with a couple of girls from her class. Because she lived the furthest away, Lou always walked the last few blocks past the park, over the railway line and down the lane to her house on her own. As she walked through the park she waited for the familiar greeting, wondering in what order Old Tom would yell his usual words today. But she didn't hear anything. When she walked around the big gum tree towards Old Tom's bench, she couldn't see him. His stuff was all there as usual, but there was no sign of him.

Must be off collecting firewood, she thought.

Lou crossed the path and walked towards the little white, wooden gate in front of the railway line. She heard the whistle of a big freight train coming around the bend. Every day she faced this same dilemma. Did she have time to run across the tracks before the train got too close or should she wait for the long train to go past? The problem was, because the freight train came at the same time every day and she knew how long it took to go past, she was always tempted to run across— if she stood and waited it took ages for the sixty carriages loaded down with grain to finally clear the crossing.

> **REMEMBER**
> We sometimes make judgments about people without thinking. When you find yourself judging someone, stop and think about why you are having mean thoughts about them. It may not be about them at all. Maybe they remind you of some part of yourself you don't like.

Standing by the gate trying to decide whether to run or wait, Lou noticed something move out of the corner of her eye. She looked down the tracks in the direction of the train and there he was. Old Tom was bent over picking up bits of broken branches from the ground alongside the tracks. *Silly old man*, Lou thought. Then she saw the train and in a split second realised that Old Tom didn't know it was coming.

'TOM,' she yelled. 'Old Tom.'

Old Tom looked up and turned towards Lou with a strange questioning look on his face. As he turned he tripped, and before Lou had a chance to yell again he'd fallen flat on his back in the middle of the tracks. Lou pushed open the little white gate and started to run towards him, yelling, 'Get up, Tom. For God's sake, GET UP!'

Old Tom was struggling to try and push himself up off the ground. Now he could see the train bearing down on him. He looked to his right and then to his left. He looked at the train then back at Lou, both racing towards him from different directions.

'GET UP!' Lou screamed.

She kept running and then she saw Old Tom look right at her—a long, sad, reflective look. He stopped struggling to get up and lay back down. The train was now only metres away. Lou could see the driver's grimacing face as he strained to pull on the brakes, his other hand sounding the horn over and over again. Lou stopped running and looked at Old Tom.

'Please, Tom,' she whispered.

Lou remembers the sound of the collision, she remembers the smell of the brakes grinding on the tracks, metal on metal. She remembers the sound of the horn blaring. She remembers the horrified look on the face of the driver as he tried in vain to stop the train. But the thing that is most vivid in her mind all day and all night is the look in Old Tom's eyes when he stopped struggling, lay back on the tracks, turned his head and just looked at her. He wasn't staring. It was like Old Tom was looking into her heart, into her mind, into her soul. Like he was hanging on to those last precious seconds in order to tell Lou something.

She'd thought about it over and over again, until she just wanted to scream. Old Tom didn't scream. He didn't even look scared. He held Lou's eyes in his and she simply couldn't look away. Their eyes seemed to be joined for ages and everything else around them seemed to be frozen in time. Then there was a flash and Old Tom was gone and the train screeched past Lou and finally stopped 50 metres down the tracks.

Lou doesn't remember how she got home. All she knows is that she ran and ran. Mum wasn't home, so she went into her room and climbed into bed. She stayed there for over a week. Every time Mum came in Lou said she was sick and couldn't get up, so Mum made her chicken soup and let her sleep. The doctor came a couple of times but never told her anything, though she heard him talking to Mum outside the door of her room.

One morning Mum came in and said, 'I'm taking you back to the doctor, Lou, you should be better by now.'

'No!' screamed Lou. She flew out of bed down the hall to the toilet and spewed. She brushed her teeth and walked slowly back to her room. Mum was sitting on her bed.

'What's going on, Lou? You need to tell me—I can't help if you don't,' Mum said softly.

'Nothing. Just leave me alone,' snapped Lou as she threw back the doona and slid into bed.

Mum took Lou back to the doctor the next week. He told her that her blood tests were all fine and he couldn't find anything physically wrong with her. Then he asked Mum if he could have a moment alone with Lou, so Mum patted her on the shoulder and left the room.

'Now, Lou, I want you to tell me what's going on. It's OK, it's just between you and me,' he said.

Lou didn't answer; she just stared at all the junk he had on his desk.

✦✦
✦ **DON'T WORRY**
When we've experienced something stressful and we don't understand
our feelings, we can think no one else will understand either. It's
important to find someone you trust to talk about it with.
✦✦✦

'Lou, this is so unlike you. Has someone at school upset
you?'

'Nup,' said Lou.

'Has anyone hurt you?'

'What do you mean?' Lou snapped.

Dr Grant spoke very softly. 'Has anyone touched you
without your permission?'

'NO! This is a bloody waste of time. You don't know
what's going on. I just want to go home,' Lou yelled.

'Righto,' Dr Grant sighed as Lou stormed out the door,
pushing past Mum. She stomped outside and sat in the car.

Lou didn't know what was wrong with her. She felt
sick, her bones ached and all she could see when she
closed her eyes was Old Tom looking at her. She thought
about it non-stop. She was puzzled. When he was looking
into her eyes she couldn't look away. Why? And how
come his eyes looked different? She could see them
clearly. They were bright blue and YOUNG looking. Had
they always been like that? She was sure when she'd
looked at him before he had old, bloodshot eyes, so
why did they look different in those few minutes before
the train hit him? And WHY did he look at her like
that? Was he angry with her for not warning him soon
enough? She didn't think so. They weren't angry eyes

that had held her own so tightly. Why wasn't he scared? 'Cause they weren't scared eyes either. Were they sad eyes? She didn't think so. She couldn't understand it. Was he trying to tell her something or was he trying to find some comfort in his last moments with the only other person there? Was it an accident or had Old Tom known what was about to happen? Had he chosen Lou? And if he had, WHY? Why didn't he just talk to her in the park?

DID YOU KNOW?

Trying to understand something when there is no easy answer can make us feel anxious and confused. If we feel anxious all the time, this can begin to have an impact on our health.

The questions rolled around and around in Lou's head. Her mind was so full of thoughts she had no room to think about what other people were saying to her, so she didn't answer. Her chest was so full of feelings she felt hot and sweaty all the time. Her heart would go from beating normally to suddenly racing the way it had when she'd run up the side of the railway tracks. Sometimes her heart just ached like someone was standing on it.

Lou was lying in her bed huddled under the doona, not knowing whether she wanted to cry or scream. Her head was thumping and she had a lump in her throat. Old Tom's eyes were holding all of her attention.

She heard a sad voice from what seemed like miles away: 'Lou? Did you hear me?'

She pushed back the doona and Mum was sitting by her bed, tears rolling down her cheeks.

'Please, Lou,' she sobbed. 'Please tell me. Is it me? Have I done something to hurt you?'

WHAT HELPED ME

'There was so much going round in my head, so many thoughts I felt like my head would explode. I just opened my mouth and let it pour out. It made no sense, but it felt better afterwards. Sort of like crying really hard but with no tears.'
Sevenya, 16

'You don't understand, Mum,' sighed Lou.

Mum hung her head. 'I just don't know what to do,' she said softly.

Lou suddenly realised this wasn't just about her. And it wasn't just about Old Tom. It was also about Mum and all the people that she loved. Shutting them out meant they were worrying like she was. They wouldn't understand, just like she didn't understand. They would all feel sick and sad like she did.

'It's Old Tom, Mum,' Lou whispered.

Mum looked confused. 'Old Tom? He's dead, Lou, he was hit by the freight train weeks ago.'

'I know,' said Lou. 'I was there.'

Q–WHAT MAKES MY WHOLE SELF?

A

There are six main elements of your whole self:

1. The physical self, your body, is made up of your senses: sight, hearing, touch, taste and smell and the parts of you that allow you to have a physical experience.

2. The psychological self, your mind, includes your memory and allows you to think, learn and process information.

3. The emotional self, your feelings, helps you to experience joy, sorrow, regret, jealousy, anger, happiness, love and all the other emotions that give colour to your life.

4. The spiritual self, the bit that searches for meaning, wants you to explore the big picture. Why are you here? What is your purpose in life? How can you make a difference? What mark can you leave on the world? What things do you value? Is there a God? What happens after you die? These are all questions that your spiritual self will explore over the course of your life.

5. The social self is shaped by your relationships and connections with people and things you value in the outside world.

6. The cultural self relates to your family, your nationality, your language, where you feel safe and where you feel included as part of a wider group. This part of you is shaped by the outside world too.

The best way to learn more about yourself as a whole person is to spend time on your own, thinking, feeling, exploring and reflecting on the things you value and feel connected to.

UNDERSTANDING THE WHOLE OF ME — — — — — — —

DID YOU KNOW?
People often think that being spiritual is about religion or faith because some of us choose to express our spiritual side through religion. But our spirit is more than what we believe—it's the essence of us, who we really are.

We may sometimes forget that there are more parts to us as human beings than just our bodies. We have a heart and mind too, and these elements are interconnected—they don't work in isolation. If this isn't complicated enough, there's our spirit as well. Our spirit gives us purpose, helping us to understand why we are here and what our role is in this lifetime. In addition to our whole being the connection of body, mind, heart and spirit, we are also influenced by what goes on in the world around us. This is the social world of relationships and the cultural world of family history—where we were born, where we live, what we eat, the songs we sing, the language we speak.

But in our internal world, the world inside us, we have ultimate control. We're in charge of how we think, feel, behave. The external world, the world outside, will have an impact on us in lots of different ways, but we can influence that world if we know ourselves well enough.

BEST MOMENT
'Sometimes I feel like I'm totally out of control, but then I just sit quietly and notice what's going on in my head. Once I pay attention to what I'm thinking, it doesn't seem so bad.'
Xavier, 13

When something bad happens in the external world, like someone we love dies or we witness something traumatic, we may need to retreat into our internal world for a while to try and make sense of this experience. When we ignore the need to look inside ourselves and think about what's going on, we may find everything starts to feel as though it's falling apart.

Once we understand that these different aspects of our being function as a whole, not in isolation, then it's easier to see why we feel bad, think weird thoughts, have physical symptoms—like vomiting, aching bones, pain etc.—and wonder about the purpose of life when we are grieving. Our heart, mind, body and spirit interact and create our WHOLE experience of grief. And that's just what's going on in our internal world.

SAD MOMENT
'I was sick of people saying to me I needed to be the "man of the house" now Dad was dead. I'm NOT the "man of the house", I'm just a kid!'
Noah, 12

The external world will also influence how we grieve. What other people say to us, how they behave and what our family does to try and make sense of the death will have an impact on us, too. This is why spending some time in our internal world can be helpful. If we understand how everything is connected to make the 'whole me', we'll understand that everything we experience is linked— mind, heart, body and spirit—and this is the key to helping us make sense of what's happening in our world, both happy and sad.

CHAPTER 11

DEAR SANTA, PLEASE GIVE ME . . . — — — — — — — — —

Andy spent every dollar he earned from his part time job on his computer. And he spent every waking hour working on his Facebook page. One night he woke up to the smell of smoke and the crackling of flames outside his bedroom door. He looked over at his little brother's bed, but it was empty.

All that week everyone had been getting ready for the fires that they knew were coming. It had been the hottest summer Andy could remember, day after day of scorching heat. It was all over the news, record after record being broken by the constant high temperatures. Worst of all, not only was it hot, but the whole country had been in a drought for more than three years. That meant there was no water to put in the pool in Andy's backyard and he couldn't even put the sprinkler on and run under that—there just was no water. The only way he had to cool off was to jump under a cold shower for long enough to get wet and then put his shorts back on without drying himself.

Andy was grateful that they didn't live in the country. His family lived in the suburbs, only 40 minutes in the car from the centre of the city. Even though there was bush around them, they called themselves city people.

The country people had been slashing grass, clearing trees and trying to save the little bit of water they had managed to collect in their rainwater tanks over the winter. And they were even keeping the water from their baths and showers and storing it in barrels, so that when the bushfires came they would at least have something to fight them with. Andy's family collected the bath water too, but Mum used it to water her roses.

'I've got no lawn left, the trees are dying and I'm not going to watch my roses die too,' she'd say as she carried bucket after bucket of sudsy water from the bathroom to the garden.

> We all value different things, things we own, things that give us joy, but sometimes when we are under threat we are forced to reconsider what it is that we truly value.

Dad thought she was crazy, but he only said that to Andy. Andy really didn't care about the garden. In fact, he wasn't really an outside sort of person. He much preferred to stay inside and chat to people on the net. Most of his friends he'd never met. They lived all over the world and he talked to them online with his webcam. His girlfriend, Chloe, lived in Paris and even though he'd never been able to touch her in person, they knew each other better than he knew the girls he went to school with. Mum was always nagging him to make 'real friends', but she just didn't understand that Andy's friends WERE real friends.

Andy shared his bedroom with his little brother, Sam, who was only five. He'd been hassling Mum and Dad for a room of his own for ages, but Mum said it was important for the boys to bond and sharing a room was a good way to do it. Andy didn't get it 'cause Sam was always asleep by the time he went to bed, so it wasn't like they talked or anything, but he'd given up asking 'cause Dad just got cross and it wasn't worth it.

At least he had a small room of his own with his computer in it. A place that was his. Andy called it 'the cave'. It used to be a storeroom, but Mum helped him clean it out when he'd bought his latest tower and monitor.

'This house is turning into a control room,' she said, happy to go along with it when Andy suggested cleaning out the storeroom. 'The cave' became Andy's refuge, the place he could go to be alone, to chat on the net and to talk quietly on his webcam to Chloe and his other friends.

That night before Andy went to bed he was watching the late news on telly with his dad. Mum had gone to tuck Sam in and read him a story.

'Looks like tomorrow's gonna be nasty,' Dad said as they watched the pictures of fires roaring through the tops of trees and jumping across roads.

'The fireys will sort it, though, won't they, Dad?' Andy asked.

'Guess so, Andy, but I tell ya what. I'm glad we don't live in the bush. Those poor blighters are in for a hell of a few days. They just said the wind could reach 130 kilometres an hour tomorrow. Could be REAL nasty.'

'Why don't they just pack up and leave then . . . You know, go somewhere safe?'

'That's easy for us to say, mate, we're here. Those poor buggers have animals, cattle, sheep and stuff to look after.

That's without all their homes and farm equipment. Some of that equipment is worth a fortune and they're already strugglin' 'cause of the drought. Hell of a position to be in,' Dad said as he leaned over to flick the fan on.

'Still bloody hot!' he said.

Andy couldn't bear to watch any more of the news. Every story seemed to be about disasters: fires, storms, droughts, floods. It seemed like the weather was going crazy. *Probably all 'cause of global warming*, he thought.

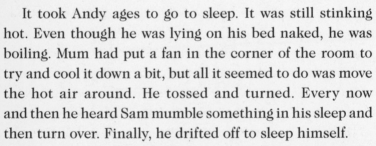

 SAD MOMENT

'We all knew the fires were coming, but it seemed to take ages. Living day by day with the threat was as bad as fighting the fires when they finally came.'
Evan, 17

It took Andy ages to go to sleep. It was still stinking hot. Even though he was lying on his bed naked, he was boiling. Mum had put a fan in the corner of the room to try and cool it down a bit, but all it seemed to do was move the hot air around. He tossed and turned. Every now and then he heard Sam mumble something in his sleep and then turn over. Finally, he drifted off to sleep himself.

It was the smell that woke Andy. An acrid, smoky smell. But it was the noise that roused him from his dreamy state. A roaring wind, like the house was in the middle of a cyclone. Then a crackling sound, like millions of twigs being snapped all at once. He looked over to see if Sam was awake, but his bed was empty. Andy flew out of bed and flicked the light switch, but nothing happened. He opened the curtains, and even though he knew it was the middle of the night it was bright outside, but not a sunny brightness—there was an eerie red glow settled over the sky and the trees were all bending in the wind.

Andy threw open the door of his room and ran down the hall to Mum and Dad's room.

'Mum, Dad, get up . . . quick, something's going on,' he yelled as he shook his dad, who was fast asleep.

'What? What?' Dad said sleepily.

Mum had heard Andy come in and was already grabbing her dressing gown.

'Quick, I think the street's on fire, Dad,' Andy said anxiously.

Dad flew out of bed and opened the curtains.

'We need to get out of here. Where's Sam?' he asked as he pulled his shorts and T-shirt on.

'I don't know, Dad, he's not in his bed.'

'Oh God, Sam . . .' gasped Mum as she raced out of the room and down the hall.

'Sam, SAM!' she was yelling.

'What will we do?' Andy asked.

'Stay here and DON'T MOVE. I'll get Sam and your mother and then we're going.'

Dad raced out of the room. Andy stood in his parents' bedroom alone. The wind was roaring and the red haze in the street was glowing brighter and brighter. He walked over to the window and looked out. He couldn't see much 'cause there was smoke everywhere. In between the gusts of wind he thought he saw the house across the road glowing red, but he didn't know if he was imagining it or not. All of a sudden he thought about his stuff. *My hard drive,* he thought and ran out of his parents' room, heading to 'the cave'. He ran into Mum in the hall; she was screaming, 'SAM! SAM!' as she opened cupboard doors, stuck her head inside, looked around and closed them again. She looked up at Andy, sheer panic on her face, tears streaming from her eyes.

'I can't find him, Andy. I CAN'T FIND HIM,' she yelled. 'Help me . . .'

Andy stood still. Time was running out, he knew it. He could hear the sound of trees burning and falling now, he knew they needed to go or they'd all be trapped. If he could just grab his hard drive, then he could find Sam and they could all get out together.

REMEMBER
What would you do? Sometimes we put our lives at risk for material stuff. Things can always be replaced, but people can't.

'Don't worry, Mum, I'll find him,' he said and ran off down the hall towards the lounge. He stopped as he reached the door of 'the cave'. *It'll only take a sec to disconnect it and put it in my bag, then I can find Sam*, he thought. He was just about to open the door to his refuge when Dad came flying around the corner.

'What the hell are you doing? I told you to stay in the bedroom,' he snapped.

'Looking for Sam, Dad. Mum can't find him.'

'Leave Sam to ME. Grab your mother and get back to the bedroom. Get the water bucket from the bathroom.

WHAT CAN HELP

Everyone should have a Home Fire Escape Plan.
Do you have one? If you don't, look at your local fire safety website, listed below, and talk to your family about how you would deal with a fire in your home or neighbourhood.

ACT Fire Brigade: www.firebrigade.act.gov.au
ACT Rural Fire Service: www.rfs.act.gov.au
NSW Fire Brigade: www.fire.nsw.gov.au
NSW Rural Fire Service: www.bushfire.nsw.gov.au
Northern Territory Fire and Rescue Service (NTFRS): www.fire.nt.gov.au
Queensland Fire and Rescue Service: www.fire.qld.gov.au
Rural Fire Service (Qld): www.ruralfire.qld.gov.au
Country Fire Service (SA): www.cfs.org.au
South Australian Metropolitan Fire Service: www.samfs.sa.gov.au
Tasmania Fire Service: www.fire.tas.gov.au
Fire and Emergency Services Authority of Western Australia (FESA): http://fesa.wa.gov.au
Country Fire Authority (Vic.): www.cfa.vic.gov.au/index.htm
If you live outside Australia, google 'Fire services' for contact details of your local fire authorities.

Wet as many towels as you can and put them around the doors and windows. Right?' he snapped. 'ANDY—you hear me? GO. NOW! And don't move from the bedroom till I get back.' Without another word Dad turned around the corner and was gone.

Andy stood at the door of 'the cave'. *It would only take me a couple of seconds*, he thought. He put his hand out towards the door handle, but before he could turn it he heard a strange sound, like a dog whimpering, coming from the linen cupboard. He started to turn the handle and then he heard it again. Then there was a giant crashing sound and he heard his mother scream.

Andy let go of the handle and leaned his ear against the door of the linen cupboard.

'Help, please help,' a sobbing, whimpering voice called. Andy threw open the door and there huddled in the very back on the bottom shelf of the cupboard was Sam.

'Come on, bro, quick, out of there,' Andy pleaded. He reached his hand into the cupboard and dragged Sam clear of the sheets and towels where he had been hiding.

'Fill your arms with towels, Sam, grab as many as you can,' he said, pulling towels in big bunches from the cupboard onto the floor. He picked up as many as he could hold and led Sam down the hall to his parents' bedroom. Andy closed the curtains and dragged Sam by the hand into the ensuite. He put the plug in the bath and turned on the cold water tap. He lifted Sam into the bath and threw all the towels in with him.

'Now listen, mate, you need to wet all these towels for me, OK?' he said, feeling himself start to panic. Mum wasn't in the bedroom and he had no idea where Dad was. They were probably still looking for Sam. Should he leave Sam here and try to find them? As soon as this thought entered his head, he knew the answer. Dad had told him not to leave the bedroom, so he would know that's where he was. He needed to stay here with Sam, and do the best he could.

Sam soaked the towels in twos and threes and Andy stuffed them around all the windows and doors. The roaring wind and crashing trees were so loud now that he had to

---

WHAT CAN HELP
When we are under threat, it can be hard to think straight.
Stopping for a moment, taking a deep breath and focusing on what
you need to do can make things clearer in your mind.

---

yell at Sam and still he couldn't hear what he said back.
The smoke was starting to come in around the windows.
Andy was really scared now. *What the hell do I do?* he
thought. He tried to remember what he'd been told when
they had fire safety training at school. 'Block the doors and
windows with wet towels. Get into a safe, low place, cover
yourself with wet towels and wait it out.' He was sure there
was something else. He couldn't quite remember, and then
it struck him: the fire extinguisher. There was one on the
wall in the kitchen. Should he risk it?

He made sure Sam was covered with cold towels and
left him sitting in the bath.

'I won't be a sec, Sam, I'll just grab the fire extinguisher.'

'No, Andy, NO!' Sam yelled. 'DON'T GO . . . PLEASE.'

Andy didn't know what to do. The fire extinguisher
might help, but then it would only last for a few minutes.
If he opened the ensuite door, the fire might find them.
Then he remembered something else they'd learned at
school. He put his hand against the door. It felt hot. *Better
stay here then*, he thought.

Andy climbed into the bath next to Sam. He covered
himself with the last of the wet towels. Sam screamed and
Andy put his arms around him, pulling him close.

'It's OK, Sam, I'm here,' he yelled. But it wasn't OK. He
had done all he could and now they just had to wait. Wait

DID YOU KNOW?
Even professional people who know what to do in an emergency experience anxiety when they are under threat. This is a natural reaction and is part of the fight-or-flight response to danger.

to be burned alive or for the fire to pass over the top of them. Andy was so scared that he wet himself.

Alby Gresham had been a fireman for forty years and he'd never experienced a fire like it. Roaring fireballs jumped from tree to tree, lighting up houses in the middle of the suburbs, fed by wind gusts that nearly blew a standing man over. They'd been fighting the fire for hours when it finally passed out of their zone and into the hands of the fresh blokes flown in from interstate. Now Alby's team had to search the houses that were still standing for survivors and put out the fires that were still burning. They moved slowly from house to house in Wishart Street. Three had burned to the ground, one was still standing, one was still on fire and one was hardly touched. Bizarre. Even after all these years, he knew it often just came down to luck.

You could prepare all you liked but at the end of the day, if Lady Luck isn't on your side you're buggered, he was thinking as he knocked down the smouldering front door of number 32.

'We've got a lady in the car here, Boss,' he heard one of his blokes yell as the door fell off its hinges. He didn't bother to ask if she was alive—he knew his boys wouldn't bother telling him if she was, they'd just radio for the ambos.

Alby walked down the hall of the house. Apart from the smoke damage and soot everywhere it seemed OK. He stuck his head into rooms one at a time. The kitchen was pretty wrecked but the lounge room seemed all right. He stuck his head into what he thought was a storage cupboard, but was surprised to find it full to the brim with computer equipment, monitors, leads, cameras . . . or that's what they had been. The heat had simply melted them all into a giant plastic river that was now starting to harden.

Finally, he knocked down the door of the master bedroom and, looking around, spotted a person hunched in the corner. He raced over and felt the man's pulse, then checked that he was breathing. *Beauty*, he thought, and got straight on to his radio.

'We need the ambos here, Cliff, over.'

'En route, Boss, over and out.'

Alby turned him onto his side and sat down next to him to wait for the paramedics to arrive. He was checking for injuries when he heard crying, or at least it sounded like crying, coming from behind a door at the far side of the room.

'Back in a minute, mate,' he said and headed towards the door.

He grabbed his axe, and with one massive swing knocked the door off its hinges. The crying changed to hysterical screams. He looked into the corner of the room and huddled in the bath, covered with black soot and towels, was a lump.

'It's OK, I'm here to help,' he said as he gently lifted the towels off the two kids still clinging together in a half full bath of water.

Q–WHAT DO YOU VALUE?

A

Do we ever stop and think about the things we truly value? It's tempting to just let life drift along without asking ourselves important questions, but now may be a good time to do this. Look at the questions below—you might like to write your answers down. Remember there is no right or wrong answer. These questions are about allowing yourself to explore the things that make your life meaningful.

If you wrote a list of presents that you want for Christmas or your birthday, what would be on it?

If you had to leave your house forever and you only had five minutes to pack a bag, what would you put into it?

If you had to escape to another country and could only take five things with you, what would they be?

If you had to choose ten people to escape with you, who would they be?

Who are the five most important people in your life right now?

What would you say to each of these people if they were about to die?

Who are the people you love the most? Why?

What are the top three things you are the most grateful for?

What parts of your life would you most miss if they were taken away?

What can you do right now to make sure the people you love know how you feel?

Once you've thought about these questions and written down your answers, you may want to make some changes in your life. Writing a plan of what you will do may help you get started. Keeping a journal of what happens over the next few weeks and months may help you keep track of how your thoughts, feelings and actions have changed.

WHEN OUR WORLD TURNS UPSIDE DOWN — — — — — —

The PlayStation, computer or DVDs we put on our Christmas list are generally not the things in life that we value the most. But sometimes we don't realise this until it's too late.

We all have basic needs that have to be met for us to survive: air, food, water and shelter are the main ones. Once these physical needs are met we focus on other things, like being safe and secure and living in an environment where we feel supported. When we feel secure our next urgent need is for love and a sense of belonging, which includes being connected to others, our relationships with family, friends and community.

We all have higher needs too. These higher needs we have are for feeling good about ourselves, being able to achieve what we want in life like doing well at school, being able to have the career we want and making a difference in the world.

And, finally, once all of these basic and higher needs have been met we need to feel good about our spiritual self, finding purpose and meaning in our life.

At each stage in our development there are things we can do to make sure we are meeting all our needs. Often we think that material possessions can make us feel safe, loved or respected by others, but when our very lives are threatened our focus shifts back to the basic needs of air, food, water, shelter and safety—because without these things we will die.

It's easy to forget the importance of our basic needs because we take food, water, shelter and safety for granted

—unless we've been hungry, thirsty, homeless or under constant physical threat. When we're unexpectedly placed in a dangerous, life-threatening situation we have to quickly rethink our values. There's no point in running in to save a computer if we die in the process.

After the danger is over and we are safe, the impact of the loss of people, home, material possessions and the life we knew can be overwhelming. We grieve for those who have died but we also grieve for what we've lost forever from our old life: our home, toys, pets, computers, equipment and community. We can always replace a house or our possessions, but we can't replace family, friends and community and we can't recapture the life we had before.

SAD MOMENT

'I felt bad 'cause I was angry that we'd lost everything, but at least we were alive. Other people had family die in the fires. Then I felt guilty 'cause we were all safe, but I was still sad. I loved our home, and all that was left was the chimney. Everything we owned was gone.'
Brianna, 14

CHAPTER 12

HELPING A FRIEND WHEN THINGS ARE TOUGH — — — —

Micky and Ben were best mates. Lately Ben had been a bit weird and Micky didn't know how to help him. Every time Micky asked 'You right there, Ben?' he would just nod and not say anything. Micky knew things weren't good at home and that Ben's mum and dad fought a lot, but something had happened lately that seemed to make it worse. Micky'd also noticed that each day at lunchtime Ben just chucked his lunch straight into the bin, which was also weird 'cause Ben was the hungriest dude Micky knew.

Micky liked most people. He had lots of friends and he seemed to be able to get on with almost anyone, but he couldn't stand Ben's dad so he avoided him. Micky remembered the first day he went to Ben's to play when they were both little. Ben's family were really rich and Micky couldn't believe how big their house was. Every room seemed to have a TV and there was a huge pool in the backyard. Ben's dad came home from work while Micky and Ben were in the garage playing with the train set. He got out of his big, shiny car and slammed the door.

'What's HE doing here?' Ben's dad snapped.

'This is my friend, Micky, Dad,' said Ben.

'Hello Mr Jackson,' Micky said shyly.

'Don't break anything!' Mr Jackson mumbled as he walked through the door into the house and slammed it behind him.

> **DID YOU KNOW?**
> It's always good to trust your instincts. If someone makes you feel uncomfortable or scared, talk to an adult you trust about it.

Ben's dad was always angry and Micky soon learned to visit Ben's when he wasn't around, which meant that they mostly hung out at Micky's house. Micky's house was small and noisy. He had four brothers and sisters and three dogs, and there was always something happening. Every room seemed to be stuffed full of people and animals, toys and books. People constantly seemed to be coming and going but Mum said 'There's always room for one more' whenever Micky asked if Ben could stay the night.

They never stayed at Ben's house. Ben had asked his mum once if Micky could stay, but she'd said, 'You know how your father is, Ben. I don't think so.' And so he'd never bothered to ask again.

That was all years ago now and the boys had got used to the way things were. It always seemed a bit odd to Micky that Ben had that huge house and all the stuff he could possibly want, but he preferred to be at his crowded little house in Finton Street kicking the footy around in the backyard. Even in the summer, Ben never swam in his own pool but came over to Micky's and they'd go to the public pool and jostle for space with everyone else. One day Micky asked Ben why he didn't swim in his pool at home.

'Dad doesn't like noise,' he said, so Micky never asked again.

Even though Ben and Micky were such good friends, there were things that they never talked about. Ben often missed school for days at a time. Last year when he came back after a week off, his arm was in plaster. Micky asked him what happened and Ben said, 'Just me being clumsy again.' Micky always wondered about that 'cause Ben was never clumsy at school. He played footy and basketball and was a great athlete, yet he always seemed to be clumsy at home. Since last year he often came to school covered in bumps and bruises. Maybe he'd get a chance to talk to Ben a bit on the school camp, Micky thought.

REMEMBER
If you're ever worried about a friend's safety, talk to an adult you trust. This doesn't mean you're dobbing.

The night before camp, Micky rang Ben to see if he could borrow a backpack.

'Sure, Mick, I'll bring one over. You around—' but before Ben could finish Micky heard Mr Jackson yelling in the background.

'Pig . . . he's just a filthy pig,' Ben whispered into the phone.

'Everything OK, Ben?' Micky asked.

'Gotta go, I'll catch ya later,' and Ben hung up.

Micky waited for ages but Ben didn't come over. He called his mobile a couple of times but the calls kept going to message bank. Micky flopped down on the couch in front of the TV.

'Everything OK, Mick?' his dad asked.

'It's just Ben. Don't know what's going on with him, Dad. He's acting really weird,' he mumbled.

Dad looked up from the newspaper. 'What sort of weird?' he asked.

'I dunno, Dad. They're a weird family. Mrs Jackson never says a word, and Mr Jackson's just a bastard.'

'Don't say that, Mick,' his dad said sternly. 'Abusing the man won't solve anything.'

'Sorry. It's just that . . . well, he's scary. He's always angry and yelling. I don't know how Ben stands it.'

Dad put the newspaper down and looked directly at Micky. 'What do you mean he's scary?'

'I just don't trust him,' Micky said.

'Well, son, he does have a pretty high-flying job. Maybe he's a bit stressed or something?' said Dad.

'Dad, you're not listening, he's ALWAYS like that,' Micky snapped impatiently. He didn't want to talk about it any more.

'Well, there's not much you can do about it, Mick. Just be around for Ben if he wants to talk.' Dad looked back down at the newspaper but then seemed to have another thought.

'He's not hurting Ben, is he, Mick?' he asked.

'Of course he's hurting him, Dad. He's mean to him all the time, he never lets him make a mess or even swim in that humongous pool they've got 'cause he doesn't like noise!' Micky said over his shoulder as he left the room.

Ben wasn't at school the next morning. The bus waited an extra half an hour while Mrs Burner, the science teacher, tried to ring Ben's mum.

DON'T WORRY

Because we are whole people, made up of the psychological, emotional, spiritual and social components as well as the physical part, we can be just as hurt emotionally and psychologically as we can physically. If someone we care about is constantly mean to us or tells us that we're fat or stupid or lazy all the time, this can hurt as much as if they hit us.

'We can't wait any longer, we need to get going,' she told the driver. The bus pulled out of the school grounds and Micky headed off to camp without Ben. He thought about Ben a lot over the next few days. He wasn't lonely or anything 'cause he had plenty of friends to hang out with. But something was troubling Micky and he just couldn't get it out of his head. When he rang his mum the day before camp finished, he asked her if she'd heard anything from Ben.

'No, Mick, but I said "hello" to his dad at the post office the other day and he didn't answer. He just ignored me. He *is* a very strange man,' Mum said thoughtfully.

'I told you!' Micky said. 'I hope Ben's OK.'

'I'm sure he's fine, love. See you tomorrow. We all miss you, you know!' said Mum, while she made silly kissing sounds into the phone.

Micky laughed. 'Me too, Mum. See you tomoz.'

Mum had cooked a welcome home roast dinner for Micky. Mum, Dad and all his brothers and sisters were sitting around the kitchen table waiting for him to walk in the door. Finally he arrived. He dropped his bags at the back door and was bowled over by the dogs, jumping up, barking and licking him.

YOU'RE NOT ALONE

We sometimes forget to enjoy the simple things in our lives, like how important the people we love are to us.

Next time someone shows you that they love you or have missed you, notice how you feel and enjoy the feeling. This is what keeps you connected to them.

'He's home,' yelled his little sister Maggie as she threw her arms around his legs and hugged him tight.

'Easy there, tiger,' said Micky, patting her on the head.

Maggie grabbed his hand and dragged him into the kitchen. 'Surprise!' they all yelled together. Mum and Dad hugged him and Mum said, 'Ooh, we've missed you, Mick!'

'Mum, I've only been gone a week,' he laughed.

'A week's a long time for a mother,' she said, ruffling his hair and pushing him towards his chair. 'Sit! Sit and eat before it gets cold,' she said.

Micky looked at the smiling faces around the table. Dad winked and nodded his head and the little kids fired questions at him all at once. Micky smiled. It *was* good to be home.

Micky didn't hear from Ben over the weekend, and every time he called his home phone or his mobile it just went to the recorded message. Finally Micky thought, *Bugger it, he can ring me*, and didn't try again.

When Micky went back to school on Monday, Ben wasn't there. He didn't come all week. He didn't come the following week either. Micky didn't know what to do. He was cross with Ben 'cause he didn't answer his calls or

REMEMBER
Try to avoid making judgments about why someone is behaving in a certain way 'cause you might be jumping to the wrong conclusions.

texts and he hadn't even been on Facebook or MSN. But he was worried too. Ben was his mate and he had a terrible feeling something was wrong. That night after dinner, he was helping Dad stack the dishwasher.

'Dad, can we talk?' he asked.

'Of course, Mick, what's on your mind?' said Dad.

'It's Ben,' Micky said.

Micky had a long talk to his dad and decided he'd go over to Ben's and see what was going on. Dad had offered to go with him, but Micky wanted to do this on his own. He rang the bell on the intercom next to the big brass front door then stood and waited. Finally a small, timid voice said, 'Yes?'

'It's just me, Mrs Jackson, Micky,' he said. She didn't answer, then Micky heard a small click and the door swung open. Micky walked into the big entrance foyer; the marble tiles felt cold on his bare feet. Mrs Jackson was standing in the doorway of the sitting room.

'Ben's in here,' she said, inclining her head towards the room they were never allowed to go into. Micky felt anxious. This all seemed like something from a cop show on TV. What was he going to find in the sitting room? A corpse? Mr Jackson with an axe?

Don't be ridiculous, he told himself as he edged his way towards the door. He rounded the corner and looked into the room. There was Ben on the sofa—he looked terrible.

Micky raced over to his friend, and as he sat on the ground next to the sofa Mrs Jackson left the room.

'What the . . .?' he asked Ben.

'I hate that pig. I hope he dies,' Ben said.

WHAT HELPED ME
'Just knowing I could talk to my best friend was the thing that helped the most. She didn't try to make me feel better, she just listened.'
Ruby, 16

'Who?' Micky asked and then it dawned on him. As he looked at Ben's bruised face, his broken leg and the bandages on his arm, it all started to make sense.

'Not your . . .'

'Yep, bastard pushed me down the stairs. Been in hospital for weeks. Just got out today. Sorry, mate, had no way of letting you know,' Ben muttered and then he did something Micky had never seen him do before: he started to cry.

'Jesus, Ben . . .' Micky stammered. He didn't know what to say. Then he had a thought that made him panic. 'He's not here?'

'Nope, disappeared weeks ago,' said Ben. 'Morning of the school camp. No one's heard from him. Cops reckon he's hiding out, the wuss.'

'The COPS?' asked Micky.

'Mum saw it this time, couldn't very well say I'd imagined it when she *saw* him do it, could she?' Ben lowered his eyes to try and stop the tears.

'He's done it before?' Micky asked, but as soon as the words came out of his mouth he remembered all the bumps and bruises, the broken arm, the stitches and everything made sense.

WHAT CAN HELP

When a friend is telling you something painful, try not to make it about YOU. So avoid saying things like 'I should have . . .' or 'I could have . . .' and concentrate on listening to what they are telling you. Stay focused on THEM.

'Ben, why didn't you tell me? Maybe I could have helped.'

'What could you do, Mick? I told Mum and she said I'd made it up. Maybe you wouldn't have believed me either,' he said sadly.

''Course I'd have believed you, you idiot. I've always been scared of your dad,' said Micky.

Micky's mind was racing. Had this been happening since they were little? If only he'd known, he could have told Dad and his dad was a big bloke, he could've sorted out weedy Mr Jackson. He could have told the cops. He could have told Mrs Burner or Dr Barrington at the clinic . . .

Ben interrupted his thoughts. 'It's not your fault, Mick.'

'I could have DONE something,' Micky said sadly.

'You did,' said Ben. 'Whenever I was at your place, I felt safe. I knew he couldn't hurt me there.'

'But maybe . . .' Micky started to think out loud.

'MICKY,' Ben snapped. 'Listen to me! If it hadn't been for you, I don't know what I would've done. I'd thought

about everything: running away, poisoning him, even . . .
even topping myself, but I didn't, 'cause of you.'

☺
BEST MOMENT
'Just being able to TELL someone how I felt was such a relief.
It didn't change what had happened, but it meant I didn't have
to do it all on my own.'
Jasper, 15
☺

Ben and Micky talked way into the night. Micky texted
his mum and told her he'd explain things when he got home.
Ben told Micky about how the years of fights and arguments
between his mum and dad suddenly became about him. As
soon as he started to grow up, his dad had become even
more angry. And he talked about the first time his dad hit
him. Micky listened in disbelief. How had he not known?

WHAT CAN HELP
Try to avoid blaming yourself for a friend having a hard time.
The important thing is to value the love and support you have in
your life and to share this with your friend. This is the best way
to help them and you.

Three weeks later the cops found Mr Jackson's body.
He'd fallen off a building in Kuala Lumpur. Ben said they
didn't know if he'd jumped or was pushed.

'At least I'm not a suspect,' said Ben cynically. 'I was
here with my leg in plaster.'

Micky thought things would be easier for Ben once his dad was dead, but surprisingly things seemed to get worse. One minute Ben said he hated his dad and was glad he was dead. Then he burst into tears and said, 'But he was my dad, MY DAD!'

Micky tried to say the right thing, but every time he agreed with Ben, Ben would change his mind and get angry. So in the end Micky just gave up saying anything and began to listen. He listened to the same stories over and over and every time he found out a little bit more about how Ben felt, what he thought and all the things that had happened to him over the years. It made Micky feel sad. All those years poor Ben had put up with his dad treating him like crap and he'd never said anything, never asked for help.

Micky thought about how lucky he was 'cause his dad was always there for him. Of course he got into trouble every so often but Dad never abused him and never, ever hit him. He could always talk to Dad about stuff that was on his mind. Ben had never had that. Ben's life had been a misery and Micky had never realised.

REMEMBER
If you don't feel safe at home always tell someone. An adult you trust like a teacher, doctor or next door neighbour is a good place to start. Everyone is entitled to live in a safe environment. Physical violence does not happen because you deserve it. It happens because the violent person has problems. It's not your fault and you don't have to be embarrassed about it.

Contacting domestic violence support services can also help. They will know how to listen and support you.

Australian Capital Territory
Domestic Violence Crisis Service
24-hour telephone counselling and referral
(02) 6280 0900

New South Wales
Domestic Violence line
24-hour telephone support and referral
1800 656 463 (TTY: 1800 671 442)

Northern Territory
Domestic Violence Crisis Service
Darwin, Mon–Fri, 9am–5pm
(08) 8945 6200

Crisis Line
24-hour general crisis counselling
1800 019 116

Queensland
Domestic Violence Telephone Service
1800 811 811 (TTY: 1800 812 225)

South Australia
Domestic Violence Crisis Service
Telephone and face-to-face counselling, referral to safe accommodation
1300 782 200 (24 hours)

Domestic Violence Helpline
Telephone counselling and information about services for those affected by abuse or who are troubled by their own behaviour
1800 800 098 (24 hours)

Tasmania
Domestic Violence Crisis Service
Mon—Fri 9am—midnight, weekends 4pm—midnight
(03) 6233 2521 or 1800 633 137

Western Australia
Crisis Care Unit
24-hour crisis support (violence, child protection, suicide, etc.)
(08) 9325 1111 or 1800 199 008 (TTY: (08) 9325 1232)

Victoria
Domestic Violence Resource Centre
www.dvirc.org.au/
GriefLine Grief Telephone Counselling Helpline
Counselling daily, 12 noon—3am
(03) 9596 7711

If you live outside Australia, google 'domestic violence support' to
get contact details for services close to you.

Q—WHAT CAN I DO WHEN NOTHING SEEMS TO HELP?

A

When we're trying to support a friend who has had a hard time, we can sometimes feel helpless. We might try a whole stack of different things, but nothing seems to work.

When we feel like nothing is working, we need to ask ourselves a few questions. Things like:

★ What am I trying to do?
★ Why am I trying to do this?
★ Are there other ways of approaching the problem?
★ Have I told my friend I don't know what to do?
★ Have I asked my friend what I could do that would help?

The reason for asking ourselves these questions is because sometimes what I think might help my friend could be totally different from what my friend thinks. I might think it helps to comfort my friend if they are crying and so will hug them and try to stop the crying, but my friend might actually feel more comfort from being able to cry for ages in my company.

The thing to remember is: if you feel that whatever you are doing to help is not working, you're probably right. The best way to understand what your friend needs is to ask them.

WHAT HELPED ME

'I felt so sad, so miserable, so hurt and everyone kept trying to cheer me up. I didn't want to be happy, I needed to feel sad.

My friend told me she didn't know what to do to make me feel better. I told her if she stopped trying to make me feel better, that would help. And it did.'

Vicky, 16

LOVE AND HATE — — — — — — — — — — — — — —

You can love someone because they're part of you, but you can hate their behaviour. And you can love someone, but that doesn't mean you always have to LIKE them. When we find ourselves in an environment where we don't feel safe we can be too embarrassed or scared to tell someone else about it, particularly if we are being hurt by someone we should be able to trust.

If we don't have an opportunity to talk about our feelings it can leave us feeling confused. We can swing from wanting to love the person to hating them. All we want from them is love, and when we don't feel loved by them it can make us angry. When someone who has hurt us dies, this makes grieving more difficult. We may feel relieved that they're dead and can't hurt us any more but then we feel sad that we haven't had the opportunity to have a happy relationship with them. This is called 'ambiguity', loving the person and hating them at the same time.

? DID YOU KNOW?

If you have feelings of ambiguity about someone who has died, you can talk to a counsellor who specialises in helping with this. See Places you can go for more information on page 181.

Lots of people have this experience, so you are not weird or unusual. ?

In this situation people sometimes withdraw into themselves, away from the outside world to a place where they feel safe, where no one can hurt them.

SAD MOMENT

'I knew my friend felt so bad and I really wanted to make it better, but I felt helpless. The more I tried to help the worse I felt 'cause nothing was working.'

Brooke, 14

When a friend suddenly seems to act differently, it's hard to know what to do. You want to help, but how can you help when you don't know what's wrong and they won't tell you? Nagging them to explain what's going on can just push them further away. You may be the only person they trust, so it's important to stay close to them until they are ready to talk about it.

If you notice a friend is behaving in a weird way, it's important to tell someone who can help: a parent, teacher or adult you trust. Tell them why you're worried about your friend and ask for their advice.

If your friend is sad, trying to cheer them up will make things worse. When you are feeling sad you need time to experience the sadness in order to make sense of it. A real friend will be with you when you are sad and not try to change how you are, no matter how uncomfortable it might make them feel.

Things you can do to support a friend:

★ Don't hassle them to talk if they don't want to.

★ Be guided by what they do want to do; if they want to be alone, that's OK.

★ Listen, even if they tell you the same story over and over again.

* ★ Don't try to fix how they are feeling by distracting them.
* ★ When a friend is sad, let them be sad. If they need to cry, let them cry as often as they need to.
* ★ Don't try to justify the actions of other people. Don't say things like, 'I'm sure he didn't mean to hurt you.'
* ★ Do show that you care by saying things like, 'That must have been really awful for you.'
* ★ Always tell an adult you trust if you think a friend is being physically or emotionally abused.

CHAPTER 13

STEPH'S FUNERAL — — — — — — — — — —

Steph had a fit on her sixteenth birthday. She doesn't remember much about it, only that in the middle of her party she felt dizzy and then nothing. She woke up later in hospital. Mum was sitting by her bed.

'How ya feeling, Steph?' asked Mum nervously.

'Got a rotten headache,' she said and closed her eyes, hoping it would go away. But it didn't. 'What happened?' Steph asked.

'Doctor says you had a seizure,' said Mum.

'What??'

'A seizure, Steph,' Mum said again.

'Let's leave it now, Mum, head's killing me, I just wanna sleep,' Steph said. And she did.

YOU'RE NOT ALONE
When someone is told they have a serious illness, it's always a shock. Sometimes they try to protect the people around them by being brave, when really they are scared and need someone to talk to about it.

That was six months ago. Steph remembered how upset Mum had been in the hospital 'cause the doctors thought she had epilepsy. But she didn't have epilepsy at all, she had a brain tumour. The radiologist said it was as big as an apple. The oncologist said it was all tangled around her brain like an octopus. Steph imagined it weaving its deadly tentacles around her blood vessels, invading her memory, her balance and growing into her optic nerve, the nerve that made her right eye see.

She went to see the surgeon and he drew an ugly tangled picture with a big black texta on his whiteboard. The more tentacles he drew the more Steph could feel them growing inside her head, like some invisible alien sucking her ability to think.

'Can't you just cut it out?' she asked.

'Sorry, Steph, it's just too messy in there. Your best chance is chemo,' the doctor said.

Mum didn't say anything. Nothing at all. She just sat there and stared.

'What about these bloody headaches?' Steph asked.

'Yep, we can help with those. Some medication'll do the trick,' he said. 'I'm going to refer you to a neurologist.'

Oncologist. Neurologist. Radiologist. *Why can't these guys call themselves something that doesn't end with –ologist?* Steph thought. *It makes them sound like they work at the zoo.*

SAD MOMENT
'Hospitals can be scary places. Sick people, bright lights, machines, people with serious looks on their faces all the time. If you're not already scared you soon will be. Finding someone who will explain things can help.'
Riley, 14

Mind you, she sometimes felt like she WAS in a zoo. Just another monkey, taking a number and sitting to wait for the next –ologist to tell her more crap she didn't understand and to handball her to someone else.

Finally, after months of radiotherapy, chemotherapy, X-rays, MRIs, CT scans and nuclear medicine, she sat in Dr Lim's office one afternoon with her mum and stepdad, Peter.

'I need to refer you on now, Steph,' he said. 'You can't have any more radiotherapy.'

'Who are you sending me to NOW?' asked Steph.

'Dr Berkshire, Larry Berkshire, he's a palliative care specialist,' Dr Lim said as he wrote a note and handed it to Steph's mum.

'Well, at least he's not an –ologist,' Steph said.

DO YOU KNOW WHAT PALLIATIVE CARE IS?

Palliative care means looking after people with a terminal illness. Palliative care doctors, nurses and others are specially trained to look after people who are dying, from the moment they know they are dying until after their death. They even support families when they are grieving.

'Palliative care?' Mum asked.

'It's the only path open to us now, Suzanne,' he said kindly. He looked back at Steph.

'You'll like him, Steph, he's a nice man.'

Steph did like Dr Berkshire. She called him 'CallmeLarry' 'cause every time she asked him something and called him Doctor, he said, 'Call me Larry.'

He was the first doctor Steph had really been able to talk to. She could ask him anything and he never avoided a question or changed the subject, no matter how awful the news was. He was the first person to answer her truthfully when she asked, 'Am I going to die?'

WHAT HELPED ME

'Medical people speak a weird language. I never understood what they were talking about. One day I started asking questions and didn't stop till I understood the answer. I didn't care how bad it was. I just needed to understand.'
Paige, 15

She knew she was going to die. She'd known from the first week. Every time people looked at her X-rays or blood results, they got a weird look on their faces. Then they'd turn away and whisper among themselves, pointing at the papers in their hands and rubbing their chins. They'd look back at Steph and Mum, smile widely and tell them some long-winded story about 'margins', 'cells', 'mets' and other words that meant bugger all to the two of them. Mum acted like it must be good news 'cause she didn't understand the words, but Steph knew better.

Steph had tried to talk to Mum and Peter about dying, but they both just said, 'Don't be silly, Steph, you're gonna be fine.' But CallmeLarry had told her the truth. So Steph started to think about her funeral—the songs she wanted played, the picture that would sit on her coffin—and she began to make a list.

> ## YOU'RE NOT ALONE
> There are special home care services available to people with
> terminal illnesses so that they can die at home. Doctors, nurses,
> spiritual carers and others including volunteers are there to help
> the person and their family live comfortably.

Clare was a nurse who visited people in their homes. She worked with Larry Berkshire, so she was used to looking after people who were dying. The first time she visited Steph, though, she got a bit of a shock. Not because Steph was so thin or 'cause she had no hair, but because she got straight to the point. Clare had hardly introduced herself when Steph said, 'Clare, I've got things I need to ask.'

'Sure,' said Clare as she sat on the end of the bed, 'that's what I'm here for.'

'I can't talk to Mum, that's why I told her to go and make you a cuppa,' said Steph.

'What about your dad?' asked Clare.

'My dad hasn't been around since I was a kid,' said Steph sadly, 'but Peter's my stepdad.'

'You can't talk to him?' asked Clare.

'Nope, I think he's just trying to make Mum happy by pretending I'll get better.'

'Oh,' said Clare.

Steph and Clare talked for ages. Mum came and went with cups of tea, but every time she looked like hanging around Steph stopped talking and Mum got the hint and left the room. Steph asked Clare all the usual questions.

WHAT HELPED ME
'I needed to know about the dying. I didn't want to be grossed out by what might happen. The nurse explained it and I wasn't scared then. Dad just died quietly, no gross noises or anything, though I was prepared for them just in case 'cause she'd told me.'
Isaac, 14

Some things Clare could answer but some things she simply didn't know the answer to . . . nobody did.

'What happens when you die, Clare?' Steph asked.

'Well, your body just stops working, Steph, bit by bit, until finally your heart stops beating and your lungs stop breathing and that's when you die,' Clare said gently.

'No, I know all that stuff, Larry told me,' said Steph impatiently. 'I mean after that.'

'Sorry, Steph, I don't know. What do you think happens?' asked Clare.

'I'd like to think there's something else. That it doesn't all end when I stop breathing,' said Steph sadly.

Clare thought for a moment. She reached out and put her hand on Steph's scrawny arm. 'Me too,' she said.

REMEMBER
No one can tell you what happens after we die. People all believe different things. So long as what you believe makes sense to you, that's all that matters.

Steph spent the next few days in a haze of sleep and forgetfulness. Her mind wandered. At the start she had been angry at her brain tumour, angry at the world. But now she felt a strange sort of calm. She wasn't thinking so much about dying, she was thinking more about what she could leave behind so the world would remember she was once here. She wanted more than a headstone at a cemetery. She wanted to leave behind something that said, 'Hey world, there was once this great chick called Steph. She loved surfing and drawing manga cartoons and writing stories. She had beautiful long blond hair and a killer figure. She looked hot in bathers. She loved cats and listening to The Killers and The Streets. She loved watching *Heroes* and *Dr Who*. People loved her and she loved them. Her life was worth something even though it was short, so PLEASE DON'T FORGET HER.'

One afternoon when Clare called in to see Steph she was asleep, huddled in her bed under the doona like a little caterpillar in its cocoon waiting to become a butterfly. Clare pulled a chair over beside the bed. She tried not to wake Steph while she checked the small machine that slowly gave her the drugs she needed to stop the headaches.

'Wondered when you'd show up,' Steph said sleepily.

'Well, Steph, I'm here now. How ya feeling?' Clare asked.

'Buggered,' she said. 'Just don't seem to have any energy. Even talking makes me tired.'

'How's your list coming along?' asked Clare.

'Could use your help,' Steph said as she leaned over and pulled a decorated pink box out of the drawer beside her bed.

DID YOU KNOW?

When someone is dying they can often feel like they have no control over anything 'cause they don't have any control over the disease or the fact that they're going to die. Helping them to grab back control of their life can make them feel really alive again and can help them focus on living rather then just waiting to die.

'It's all in there, but I need you to read it through for me. Can't see a bloody thing out of this eye,' she said, pointing wildly to her right eye as it rolled around like it had a life of its own.

Clare lifted the bundle of folded papers out of the pink box. She put them in her lap and started to go through them one at a time. There was a list of songs. There were poems. There were pages and pages of stories. There were pieces cut from magazines. There were pictures of flowers. There were pen and ink drawings of big-eyed manga girls with swords and wands that reminded Clare of the Astro Boy cartoons she used to watch on TV when she was a kid.

'You seem pretty organised, Steph,' said Clare as she carefully placed the papers back into the box. 'What's the next step, do you think?' she asked, as Steph closed her eyes and looked like she was dozing off to sleep again.

'Who can I give it to, Clare?' Steph asked.

'I think the time's come for you to talk to your mum,' said Clare gently.

Steph sighed. 'Already tried,' she said. 'She doesn't wanna know. Still keeps telling me I'll get better.'

Clare looked out the window into the backyard. She was racking her brains. There has to be someone, someone in the family Steph can be honest with, she thought. Her eyes fell on to a little white and blue cross, tucked under a big tree by the garage. 'What's that cross out there by the garage, Steph?' she asked.

Steph slowly opened her eyes. 'That's Roger. I still miss him,' she said.

'Roger?' asked Clare.

'My cat,' said Steph. 'He got hit by a car years ago, too old and slow to get out of the way.'

WHAT HELPED ME

'When my dog Wombat died we buried him under the tree where he liked to sleep. I used to visit him a lot. I sat under the tree and just talked to him like I used to. It made me feel close to him.'
Sean, 13

Steph told Clare about the day Roger died and how she got her stepdad Peter to wrap him up in the bunny rug she'd had since she was a baby. Peter made a coffin out of an old shoebox and Steph painted it with flowers and stuck cartoon pictures of mice all over the lid. She told Clare about how she'd invited the neighbours to the funeral and they'd stood around the hole in the ground as Peter put the decorated box down into the earth. She also told Clare how her mum thought it was silly to have a funeral for a cat.

'Funerals are for people, Steph, and even then they're awful. I hate going to funerals,' she said.

Clare looked back out into the garden; the flowers were dropping off the big, purple jacaranda onto the grass around the little white and blue cross. She smiled and turned back to Steph.

'I've got an idea,' she said.

Steph pulled herself up onto her elbow and leaned over towards Clare. She looked deep into her eyes. 'Well?' she asked.

Clare wasn't there when Steph died, but she saw her soon after. She walked into the familiar room she'd visited so often in the past weeks. Steph was lying quiet and still. Her eyes were shut and her bald head looked almost transparent. Mum was sitting on a chair by the bed with her hand on Steph's arm. She didn't move at all when Clare walked in. Peter was sitting next to Mum with the pink box in his lap.

'Thanks for coming, Clare,' he said.

'I'm sorry I wasn't here,' said Clare as she gently leaned over the bed and stroked Steph's bald head.

'Is there anything I can do?' she asked. Mum didn't speak. She didn't even move. She just sat staring at the blank face of her little girl. No tears, no words.

WHAT CAN HELP

It's always helpful to spend time with someone you love after they've died if possible. Sitting with them, touching them, talking to them and just being with them gives you a chance to say goodbye. If you aren't able to do this, sitting in their room or on their bed—in a place where they spent lots of time—can help. Close your eyes and imagine them with you.

'It's all pretty well organised,' Peter said finally. 'Steph and I had a good talk last night. She's planned everything: the coffin, the flowers, the songs, the notice for the paper. Everything,' he said. 'It's all here. All of it, in this little pink box.'

Peter held up the box so Clare could see it. His eyes were wet with tears. He looked at Clare with a sadness that needed no words.

'Now we just have to work out how we're going to live without her,' he said.

Q–HAVE YOU EVER BEEN TO A FUNERAL?

A

Funerals are a way of saying goodbye to someone we love surrounded by other people who loved them too. Some of us might never have been to a funeral; others will have been to more than one funeral by the time they reach high school.

Back in the day, funerals were always held in churches. The coffin was placed in the centre of the church with flowers on the top. All the people who went to the funeral wore black clothes. Prayers were said, hymns were sung and it was very serious. These days there are no rules. Funerals don't have to be in a church, people don't have to wear black; in fact, they sometimes dress in the favourite colour of the person who died, so everyone might wear blue or red or green. The coffin is not necessarily at the funeral, and instead of prayers people might read poems or recite words from a favourite song.

It doesn't really matter how the funeral looks as long as it reminds people of the person who died and gives them a chance to share their sadness with others. It is a way of saying 'we love you and we will miss you'.

WHEN SOMEONE KNOWS THEY'RE DYING — — — — —

Most people, no matter how old they are, know they're dying even when no one tells them officially. People who have a terminal illness have often gone through weeks or months of treatment in the hope of slowing down or curing the disease. During this time they see and hear things that people think they haven't noticed. They see the fear and worry in the eyes of the people around them. They hear bits of whispered conversations. But above all they feel what's happening in their bodies. They see themselves getting thinner and thinner as the days go by. They notice that they don't feel hungry and that they have no strength and no energy. They notice themselves getting sleepier day by day.

The things that are important to them change. They stop thinking so much about the distant future and begin to focus on the present. They start to think about their legacy, what they are leaving behind for the people who love them. What mark they've made on the world. How they'll be remembered. Even though it can be extremely difficult, a person who's dying will often want to talk about what they're thinking and feeling to someone they trust. It can make it a very lonely time if no one around them feels comfortable having this conversation.

WHAT CAN HELP
Just be led by the person. If they say they need to talk to you, listen. Just listen. Let them say everything they need to say without interrupting or disagreeing with them. This is an important time for them and for you.

If someone you care about is dying and tries to talk to you about it there are a number of things you can do. First, never change the subject. It takes a lot of courage for the person to bring it up and they'll have been thinking about it for ages. If you change the subject or make it obvious that you don't want to talk about it, they may never get another chance. Second, if it makes you feel uncomfortable it's OK to say that, but don't deny what's happening by saying things like, 'Don't be silly, you're not going to die, you get a bit better every day.' Saying these sorts of things just makes them feel more alone.

Sometimes people say, 'I don't want them talking about dying 'cause they need to have hope.' That's true, but they need to have realistic hope. Hope of spending the time they have left with people they love. Hope of being able to do the things they think are important before they die. Hope of being able to say things they need to say to the people they love. Hope of a comfortable death. We TAKE AWAY this hope if we won't let them talk about their thoughts and feelings with us.

CHAPTER 14

THINKING ABOUT THE MAN IN THE MIRROR — — — — —

Michael Jackson died on 26 June 2009, and it had a strange impact on Oliver. He was nearly eighteen, busy studying for his final high school exams, learning to drive a car and getting ready to vote in his first election. He wasn't a kid any more and yet as soon as he heard the news on the radio that morning he felt like he'd just lost his best friend.

He'd liked Jacko's music when he was younger, but then he got into alternative music and his Michael Jackson CDs lay forgotten at the bottom of his wardrobe. Michael Jackson became 'old school', and even when he launched his final tour early in 2009 Oliver didn't even consider buying tickets—he wasn't really interested.

DID YOU KNOW?
Music can represent different things to us at different times in our lives.

But now he found himself feeling really sad and he didn't understand it. He got dressed, ate his breakfast and headed off to school. From the moment he walked through the big glass doors into the corridor at school everyone was talking about it. Some of his mates said it was a hoax and there had been plenty of them before. Others said he was weird anyway and that any fifty-year-old man who still thought he was a kid needed serious help. Oliver found himself getting angry with the kids who were saying awful things about Jacko.

'What would you know, ya wanker?' he snapped at one of the boys who was standing by the lockers bad mouthing Michael Jackson.

The red-haired boy pulled a face at Oliver as he walked past.

'Oh, you're so BAD, man!' he sniggered and all his friends laughed. Oliver turned and rushed at him. He grabbed the boy by the collar and pushed him against the locker.

'What did ya say, Ranga?' he hissed.

REMEMBER
Try to avoid losing your temper when you're feeling sad.

Sometimes people say things without thinking and if we respond on the spur of the moment we can regret it later. If you feel angry, STOP! Take a breath and think about how to respond before doing anything.

The red-haired boy shrank back, wriggling to get out of Oliver's tight grip on his neck.

'Nothin', nothin' dude, just muckin' round,' he replied nervously.

'Well don't,' snapped Oliver, letting him go and turning to walk away. He felt hot and flushed. He put his head down and continued up the corridor towards his classroom.

He was suddenly aware of someone walking along next to him, his friend Jasmine.

'What was that about, Ollie?' she asked. 'You really lost it.'

'Don't know, Jas, I just fired. That Ranga's always annoyed me.'

'He's only a kid, Ollie,' she said, but when she saw the angry look on Oliver's face she changed the subject.

'Catch you at recess?' she asked as she turned into her classroom. Oliver grunted and kept walking.

He sat through his class but couldn't concentrate. He doodled in his notebook instead of writing anything that mattered. He avoided Jasmine at recess and lunchtime, and the end of the day came before he knew it. He left school as soon as the bell rang and headed home before any of his mates could catch up with him.

When he got home he went straight to his room, dropped his bag on the floor and grabbed his iPod. He searched through his playlists until he found what he was looking for. He put his headset on and, lying on his bed, pressed play.

WHAT HELPED ME
'I sat for hours listening to the saddest music I could find. I needed to cry and couldn't, but when I put on the music I cried and cried. And then I felt a bit better.'
Sophie, 13

When Mum called him for dinner he told her he wasn't hungry. She stood at the door, smiling at him.

'You have to eat, Oliver. You need to feed your brain. Exams coming up, you know,' she said.

'I know,' Oliver snapped.

'Something up?' Mum asked.

'Nope, just want to be alone,' he said. So Mum shut the door and left him to his thoughts.

SAD MOMENT
'I felt like an idiot. I couldn't understand why I felt so sad. I had no right. I didn't even know the guy.'
Lil, 15

He felt bad for getting mad with Mum. She was just looking after him, as usual. Oliver didn't understand why he felt so crappy. He knew he had exams coming up and yet he'd wasted a whole day at school, tracked out and doodling in his notebook. He couldn't even remember if he'd written anything at all. He leaned over and pulled the notebook from his bag. He opened it and was astonished at what he saw. Pages and pages of meaningless doodles with the occasional recognisable image. A coffin here, a zombie there. Over the page was the statue from the *HIStory* album cover and a chimpanzee. The next page had lines and lines of song lyrics and a picture of a black panther.

What the hell's wrong with me? he thought as another wave of sadness swept over him. He wanted to cry but he didn't know why—it made no sense.

Oliver leaned over and grabbed the remote control to his TV. He turned it on and lay back on his bed. The sound always came on before the picture but he didn't need to see the picture: he knew the voice, the tune and the words. He should have guessed. All the channels were playing Michael Jackson tributes. That was it, the tears started to flow.

Mum pushed the door open and walked over towards the bed. Oliver wiped his eyes with a tissue.

'What's the matter, Ollie?' she asked.

'Don't know, Mum, it's all this Michael Jackson stuff, it's screwing with my head,' he sniffed.

'You feeling sad?' she asked.

'Yeah, I don't get it. It's not like I thought he was that great or anything, but I feel really awful.'

'You know, I had a similar feeling when Michael Hutchence died. I cried for days and I was never a big fan of INXS,' she said.

'Really?' asked Oliver.

'Yep. I ended up talking to my dad about it. He said he'd felt like crap when Frank Sinatra died . . . but then Dad loved him, sang his songs all the time,' Mum said.

Oliver blew his nose on the tissue.

'You're not the only one, you know. Did you see the news tonight?' asked Mum.

'Nup.'

'Well, there are people putting flowers outside his ranch and at his parents' house. People crying, singing songs and dancing the moonwalk. All dressed up with silver gloves and everything.'

'Really?' said Oliver.

'You know, Ollie, I don't think it's the person so much, it's what they represent to us,' Mum said.

'What do ya mean?' asked Oliver.

'Well, you grew up with Michael Jackson. You loved him when you were little. You used to sing his songs all the time. He's part of your childhood. Maybe now he's dead it's reminded you that you're all grown up and those days are gone.' Mum gently stroked Oliver's hair.

'But it's not like I knew him or anything. He's just someone famous,' Oliver said, trying to make some sense of all of it.

'Yeah, but I remember lots of people being really sad when Princess Diana died and President Kennedy. Elvis was another one. Oh, and Marilyn Monroe.'

'Who?' asked Oliver.

'Oh, she was well before your time, love. But it's the same sort of thing.'

Oliver didn't say anything. He was thinking about what Mum had just said.

'It's OK to feel sad, Ollie. When someone dies, whether we know them personally or not doesn't matter. It's still a reminder that our lives are moving on, we're growing older every day and eventually that will be me and you.'

'Don't say that, Mum,' Oliver pleaded.

'It's true, love, that's life,' Mum said in her matter-of-fact way. 'The most important thing is to remember the good things people did. Michael Jackson made some great music. Maybe our job is just to enjoy it.'

Mum patted Oliver on the arm and headed towards the door.

'Don't stay up too late will you, Ollie?'

'No, Mum,' he said as he put his headset back on and pressed play on his iPod.

Q—IS THERE A FAMOUS PERSON YOU FEEL INSPIRED BY?

A

It's OK to be inspired by other people. They may be artists, musicians, actors, writers, politicians, human rights activists, environmentalists, scientists or any number of other devoted individuals who work hard to make the world a better place. Sometimes we get caught up in the glitz and glamour of the celebrity lifestyles we see in the media and think we'd like to be rich and famous too. The people we truly look up to, though, are generally those who are working to achieve something greater than fame and wealth.

Who are the famous people you look up to?

Why?

Is there someone famous whose death had an impact on you?

Who was it?

How did you respond?

Did anyone else understand how you felt?

Were you able to talk about it with anyone?

WHEN SOMEONE FAMOUS DIES — — — — — — — — —

Sometimes we actually feel like we know famous people personally. We see them so much on the television and in movies, we read about the intimate details of their lives in magazines, and if they happen to be musicians we listen to their music over and over, connecting to the words they sing as if they're singing directly to us.

Music, in particular, has an enormous impact on us. It transports us to a different time and a different place just by hearing it. There is music that makes us feel happy and music that makes us feel sad, usually because we remember hearing that music in the past when that was how we were feeling at the time. In fact, an upbeat, happy song can make us feel sad if that's how we were feeling the first time we heard it. Music is an extremely powerful tool for connecting with our emotions.

We often identify with particular famous people because they represent something we aspire to. An actor you like may have inspired you to study acting. A writer you admire may have inspired you to start writing. A musician may have inspired you to learn an instrument. A social activist may have inspired you to stand up for what you believe in. But it doesn't even need to be this obvious. It may just be that a particular famous person represents to you a specific time in your life that was important. When the famous person dies, it can have a surprisingly emotional impact.

We are not alone in these responses. You only need to look at the outpouring of genuine grief by people all over the world when Michael Jackson died. Similar scenes were played out around the world with the deaths of Heath

Ledger, John Lennon, Princess Diana, Kurt Cobain, Jeff Buckley, Elvis, the Queen Mother, Bud Tingwell and Martin Luther King Jnr, to name just a few. All of these people represented different things to the people who grieved for them.

It's important to remember that if you're feeling sad when someone famous dies, that's OK. It doesn't matter that you didn't know them, they obviously played a part in your experience of life up till now. Allow yourself to feel sad, but spend some time exploring what that sadness means and what time in the past it reminds you of.

DON'T WORRY

You know when you're feeling better 'cause you can listen to the music and remember the past fondly. You can also think about the famous person in terms of their legacy (what they left behind) without feeling sad.

CHAPTER 15

I JUST WANT TO BE HAPPY! — — — — — — — — —

Millie sat in the old leather armchair. Her shoes were on the floor and her legs were tucked up in front of her. She wound her arms around her knees and held them tight. She could hear the counsellor's voice droning on and on, but she wasn't listening, she was thinking.

WHAT HELPED ME
'One day I realised I was in control. Other people can't make me feel anything unless I let them. So I began to notice my feelings and gradually I concentrated on the good feelings and let the bad ones just slip away.'
Megan, 15

Millie was sick of feeling sad. She'd had enough of the knot that tightened in her belly every time she walked into the yard at school and saw the cool girls sitting on the benches whispering about her. She'd tried to become one of their gang plenty of times and sometimes she thought she'd made it but then they'd laugh at her and walk away. The last few months had been terrible for Millie. She let her mind wander.

Her grandma died just before Christmas, and the holidays were awful. Everyone was sad, especially Mum,

✦✦
✦ **DON'T WORRY**
When someone dies, even times that are supposed to be happy
aren't. You can't distract yourself 'cause every time your mind is
quiet, you remember that the person has died.
✦✦
✦

so the family didn't go away as they usually did. They just stayed home. Mum wouldn't even take them to the beach when it was hot. She just sat around crying and Millie didn't know how to make her feel better. Then she started at a new school, and Millie had to try and make friends. It hadn't gone well. The cool kids didn't want to know her. The brainy kids talked about stuff she didn't understand. The sporty kids dumped her as soon as they realised she wasn't very sporty, so that just left the geeks and emos and she didn't fit in with them either.

Just when Millie thought things couldn't get any worse, she came home from a rotten day at school and found Dad sitting at the kitchen table with his head in his hands.

'What're you doing home so early, Dad?' she asked.

'Sit down, Mill, we need to talk,' he said softly.

Dad reached over and put his hand on Millie's arm.

'What's wrong, Dad?' she asked, though she didn't really want to know.

One look at Dad's face told Millie that something terrible was wrong.

'It's Mum,' he said, 'she's gone.'

Millie was confused. 'Gone? What do ya mean, gone?'

'She's gone, Millie. Packed up and gone. Not coming back,' said Dad sadly.

'Gone where?'

Dad said nothing. He dropped his head and sighed.

'Gone where, Dad?' she asked again.

REMEMBER

Try to avoid blaming yourself for everything that goes wrong in life. Some things you can change and some things you can't. If you can't change something, blaming yourself just makes everything worse. Writing down what's happened can help you see that it wasn't your fault.

'I don't know, she's just gone.'

Nothing made any sense to Millie. Why would Mum leave? Where had she gone? Was she coming back? Millie loved her mum but she was really angry with her. She didn't understand. Why would she do this? Why hurt Dad?

What about me? thought Millie. *Doesn't she care about me?* The same questions whirled around and around in her head. Questions with no answers. Nothing made sense.

The thoughts were bad enough but the feelings were worse. They rumbled round and round in Millie's gut. She felt sad, angry, guilty, ashamed and then angry again. Anger was the one that tied her in knots. Sometimes she felt so angry she threw things. One day she picked up the beautiful china doll Mum had given her when she was little. She stroked its beautiful, golden, curly hair and then before she knew what she was doing she smashed it against the end of her bed and shattered the pale china face into hundreds of pieces that landed all over the floor.

She sat and stared at the painted blue eye that rolled around and around before it bumped into the bookcase and stopped. The blue eye stared back at her.

WHAT CAN HELP

When you feel angry, try to find ways of dealing with it that won't make you feel sad later. Write down your thoughts, paint a picture of your feelings, do some strenuous exercise or go somewhere private and scream out loud. Anything that's not destructive and helps release the energy will help.

This was how Dad found her, huddled on her bed, surrounded by the china shards that had been the face of her doll, staring at the blue glass eye. When Dad spoke, it surprised her.

'Millie, what are you doing?' he asked as he looked around the room anxiously.

Millie blinked. She looked at the floor in horror. She jumped from the bed and started to sweep up the pieces of china with her hands.

'Careful, you'll cut yourself,' Dad blurted out as he grabbed her arm.

Millie reached over and gently picked up the blue glass eye. She held it in her fingers, turning it over and over. Suddenly she realised what she'd done and burst into tears.

Dad had a long talk with Millie that afternoon. He told her that it wasn't her fault that Mum had left. He told her that Mum still loved her and that when she had settled into her new house, Millie could go and visit. He also told

Millie that Mum had been unhappy for a long time, and when Grandma died things came to a head. But none of this helped. Millie still didn't understand and she still didn't feel any better. Nothing Dad said made the feelings go away.

SAD MOMENT
'It got so bad I began thinking about what else could go wrong. It was like I was being punished or something.'
Max, 13

'It's OK, Dad,' she said eventually. 'I'll be right.' But she hadn't felt right for ages.

The world had become a scary place. Every time she allowed herself to be a part of it, she got hurt. Her grandma left her, then her mum and the kids at school had never accepted her, so Millie spent more and more time on her own. On her own she felt safe. No one could hurt her if she was on her own. She built an invisible wall around herself and stayed inside it. She imagined the wall reaching into the sky with a tiny door and a lock that could only be opened with a special brass key. She could almost feel the key in her hand. A key she held so tightly no one could take it from her. She didn't talk to anyone except Dad, and even then only when she had to.

One night at dinner, Millie was pushing peas around on her plate with her fork. She was watching them roll around, bumping into the mashed potato and getting stuck.

She felt her dad's hand on her arm and looked up.

'Millie, can you hear me?' he asked again anxiously.

'What Dad?'

'I just said, "I've made an appointment for you to see a counsellor tomorrow".'

Millie suddenly felt nervous; she didn't know why. 'What for?' she asked.

'I'm worried about you. You need to talk to someone.' He sighed. 'I've tried, but it's not working.'

'Dad, I'm fine. I . . .' but before she could finish making up an excuse, Dad interrupted. He seemed angry.

'NO, Millie. You're NOT fine.'

And now here she was, sitting for the third time in the office of the counsellor. Letting the counsellor talk while she sat behind her invisible wall thinking. Just thinking and waiting for the session to end. The voice of the counsellor made a soundtrack for her thoughts. Pictures rolled around in her mind. Pictures and memories of when things were good. When Grandma was alive and Mum was happy.

☺ **BEST MOMENT**

'When I thought about how it used to be, I felt warm and happy. I stopped myself thinking about the crap and focused on the good feelings that the memories brought.'

Eli, 15 ☺

The voice of the counsellor stopped. Millie waited for her to start talking again, but she didn't. The silence stretched on. The longer it lasted the more the silence dragged Millie from behind her invisible wall and back into the room.

She began to feel awkward. She lifted her head and looked at the counsellor. The counsellor smiled gently, and didn't say anything. Millie wriggled around in the leather chair, feeling more and more uncomfortable as each second ticked past. Should she say something?

No! she thought. *This is a test, she's trying to get me to talk.*

So Millie just sat there, staring at the counsellor and trying to ignore the growing feeling of anxiety that was building up inside her. Finally the counsellor broke the spell. She leaned forward and looked deep into Millie's eyes.

'You're not good enough—is that it?' she whispered.

Millie felt her cheeks flush red. She felt tears prick behind her eyes. She felt the familiar anger start to knot in her gut.

'Is that it, Millie?' she asked gently. 'You don't think you deserve to be happy?'

'I don't. I'm not good enough. It's all my fault,' Millie blurted out.

The counsellor leaned back in her chair and smiled. She looked deeply into Millie's eyes. 'What makes you say that?' she asked.

Millie thought for a moment. She thought about her mum, her grandma, her dad, the girls at school. Everything at once. She opened her mouth and without even trying words started to tumble out.

Q—HOW CAN I PRACTISE HAPPINESS?

A

Here are some things you can do to practise feeling happy.

★ Write a Grateful List. Start with simple things. Read it every morning before you start your day and add something to it every night before you go to bed. Before you know it you'll become more aware of the things that happen during the day that make you happy.

★ Practise smiling. Even when you don't feel like smiling, make yourself do it and before you know it you will not have to try, you'll be smiling easily. It can help to do this in front of the mirror.

★ Do something kind for someone else every day. Don't make a big deal about it; a secret kindness— like leaving a bunch of flowers on the doorstep of a neighbour—will make you feel the happiest.

★ Stop and notice how you feel a couple of times during the day. If you find you're anxious or upset, think about something on your Grateful List, then take a few deep breaths and hold the sense of happiness that comes from being thankful—you'll be better prepared to deal with the problem that was making you upset.

Can you think of other ways you can practise happiness? Make your own list of ways to practise happiness and start practising TODAY!

MY GRATEFUL LIST

I am grateful for:

- Always having enough to eat and drink.
- Having a nice place to live.
- Being healthy.
- My family.
- My cat Greyfoot.
- The hug Mum gave me today when I came home from school.
- Finding Grandma's old clock in the garage and remembering her.
- The letter I got today from my big brother, Nick.
- The fun I had today at the beach.
- Learning to skate.
- Passing my English exam.
- Making friends with Bridie.

Milo, 13

WHAT IS HAPPINESS? – – – – – – – – – – – –

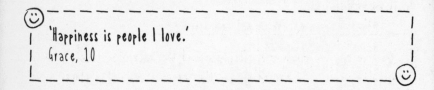

☺
'Happiness is people I love.'
Grace, 10

We all have different ideas about what being happy is and what makes us feel happy. Sometimes we spend so much time thinking things like, *If only I find a boyfriend, or get picked for the basketball team, or pass my exams, or get into uni, I'll be happy.* We spend so much time thinking about what might happen in the future to make us happy we forget to find the happiness in each minute, in each day.

☺
'Happiness is playing with my dog, Flip.'
Jane, 11

'Happiness is lying on the beach with my eyes closed, feeling the sun and hearing the waves.'
Mandy, 16
☺

Feeling happy, like everything else, is something we have to practise if we want to get good at it. Sometimes we miss things that have the potential to make us happy because we're not paying attention. We don't notice the little flower growing among the weeds. We don't notice the crazy laughter of a little kid playing in the park. We don't notice the old lady who smiles at us as we pass her in the street. We don't notice the beauty and joy of the world we live in 'cause it's like we're walking around with our eyes closed.

> 'Happiness is Christmas Eve, sitting around the decorated tree with the smell of pine needles, and the presents wrapped. I close my eyes and that's happiness to me.'
> Em, 14

When someone we love dies or leaves we may think we'll never feel happy again, but gradually over time we will begin to find joy in small things. A little bit here, a little bit there, and then one day out of the blue we suddenly realise we are feeling happy, sometimes for no particular reason. We'll remember the fun things we did with the person who died and how much we love them, and we'll feel happy. But intense happiness is not something we can feel all day, every day even when everything is going along fine. There will always be periods of feeling sad, disappointed, hurt, regretful and scared. These feelings are all a perfectly natural part of living, but if we practise happiness, even in sadness, we can find comfort.

> 'Happiness is being at the footy and hearing everyone cheer and yell when my team kicks a goal.'
> Johnny, 17

We can't depend on other people to make us happy. We might believe that if we hang out with the right crew or if we're popular we'll be happy. But being happy happens on the inside, and we are the only one who can control that. The funny thing is if we practice feeling happy on the inside and approach each day with happiness in our heart, over time the attitude of the people around us changes too. They see our happiness and want to be part of it. When you stop trying to make people like you and spend some time learning to like yourself, happiness begins to blossom.

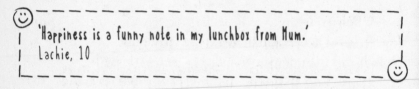

'Happiness is a funny note in my lunchbox from Mum.'
Lachie, 10

Some people think you have to be perfect to be happy, but none of us is perfect. Some people think you have to earn happiness and it's a reward for being good—they don't deserve to be happy because they're not good enough. But none of this is true. You have to learn to be happy; it's like any skill you want to acquire, you have to practise it and live it and suddenly you'll realise you had it there all along, you just weren't aware of it.

'Happiness is being in the middle of a huge crowd in the mosh pit at a concert and looking at the joy on my kids' faces as they dance and sing to the music.'
Molly, old enough to have kids!

PLACES YOU CAN GO FOR MORE INFORMATION

Grief support services

National Association for Loss and Grief: www.nalagvic.org.au, (03) 9650 3000, 1800 100 023

Bereavement Care Centre: www.bereavementcare.com.au, 1300 654 556, online programs for young people www.bereavementcare.com. au/b_u_club/bearing_up_club.htm

Australian Centre for Grief and Bereavement: www.grief.org.au, 1300 664 786

Paradise Kids: www.paradisekids.org.au/services

Rainbow grief support for kids and adults: www.rainbows.org.au, for NT, SA, WA: (08) 9221 3363, for ACT, Qld., NSW, Tas., Vic.: (07) 3844 9715

Very Special Kids: www.vsk.org.au/Bereavementsupport, Vic.: (03) 9804 6222

Griefline: www.griefline.org.au

ACROSS: www.acrossnet.net.au

For help with grief support in your local area simply Google 'grief services' and add where you live (suburb, state and country).

Palliative care services

National Palliative Care Service Directory: http://pallcare.gky. com.au/c/pc?a-apps&ap-bd

Palliative Care, Australia: www.palliativecare.org.au, (02) 6232 4433

Palliative Care, NSW: www.palliativecarensw.org.au, (02) 9206 2094
Palliative Care, Queensland: www.palliativecareqld.org.au, 1800 660 055

Palliative Care, Victoria: www.pallcarevic.asn.au, (03) 9662 9644
Palliative Care, WA: www.palliativecarewa.asn.au, 1300 551 704
Tasmanian Association for Hospice and Palliative Care: www.tas.
palliativecare.org.au, (03) 6285 2514
Palliative Care Council of South Australia Inc.: www.pallcare.asn.au,
1800 660 055

Other places that can help
Lifeline: www.lifeline.org.au, 131 114
Kids Helpline: www.kidshelp.com.au, 1800 551 800

Don't forget that you can always ask teachers, school counsellors,
your local doctor or an adult you feel comfortable with for help
to point you in the right direction.

For people who live outside Australia, simply Google words like
'death', 'grief support' or 'counselling' to find services that can
help you in your local area.